# Arts and Crafts
# ARCHITECTURE
'Beauty's Awakening'

# Arts and Crafts
# ARCHITECTURE
## 'Beauty's Awakening'

## JULIAN HOLDER

THE CROWOOD PRESS

First published in 2021 by
The Crowood Press Ltd
Ramsbury, Marlborough
Wiltshire SN8 2HR

**enquiries@crowood.com**

**www.crowood.com**

**British Library Cataloguing-in-Publication Data**
A catalogue record for this book is available from the British Library.

ISBN 978 1 78500 796 5

**Dedication**
To Holly and Jacob
with love always

**Cover images**
Front cover: Lupton Hall, Bedales, Steep; back cover: Pier Terrace, West Bay, Bridport; rear flap: (top) memorial to Detmar Blow carved by Eric Gill, St Swithun's Church, Brookthorpe, (bottom) All Saints, Brockhampton.

**Frontispiece**
Simply held together with a piece of rough string, this beautifully carved stone finial of wild roses greets visitors at the garden gate at Avon Tyrrell House, Hampshire.

Typeset by Derek Doyle & Associates, Shaw Heath
Printed and bound in India by Replika Press Pvt. Ltd.

# Contents

## Acknowledgements

As William Morris wrote 'Fellowship is life, and lack of fellowship is death' so it gives me great pleasure to acknowledge the many individuals and institutions that have helped me in one way or another including John Archer, Paul Barnwell, Sara Biscaya, Simon Blow, Geoff Brandwood, Abigail Brookes, Ian Campbell, Andrew Davison, Ian Douglas, Ian Dungavell, Stuart Evans, Andy Foster, Simon Green, Susan Halls, Alec Hamilton, Clare Hartwell, Elain Harwood, the late Richard Holder, Holly and Jacob Holder, Edward Holland, Vicky House, Jerry Hurst, Ian Johnson, Alison MacKenzie, Elizabeth McKellar, Andy Marshall, Dave Morris, Tara Murphy, Joanne O'Hara, Stephen Parissien, Jeremy Parrett, Alan Powers, Lou Rosenburg, Caroline Stanford, Neal Shasore, the late Gavin Stamp, Paul Stamper, Steve Stankiewicz, Mark Swenarton, Phil and Michael Thomas, the Society of Architectural Historians of Great Britain, the Twentieth Century Society, the Victorian Society, the Ashmolean, Blackwell, Hampstead Garden Suburb Trust, the Landmark Trust, the National Trust, New Walk Museum and Gallery, the Oxford Union, the Wilson, the Bodleian Library, Manchester Metropolitan University Library (Special Collections), Morrab Library, RIBA Library, Rewley House library, University of Sheffield Library, University of York Library (especially King's Manor), West Dean College, my editors at The Crowood Press, and finally, as ever, the Poldhu Beach café.

IT CAN BE NO ACCIDENT THAT THE ARTS AND Crafts Movement appeared just as the size of the urban population began to overtake the rural for the first time. This book takes as its starting point the observation of C.R. Ashbee that 'The proper place for the Arts and Crafts is in the country'. It is a particular point of view but one that Ashbee, amongst many, believed and one which I find increasingly persuasive. When Arts and Crafts architecture 'went to town' it changed into a very different kind of architecture. That is a separate story to the one told here. Urban life was the bogeyman of the Movement and it reacted to it in various ways. Chief amongst these was finding solace in an imaginary pre-industrial past. This refuge was sought not only to take comfort from but to set standards for improving contemporary life by looking back to a more humane architecture – and the type of society that produced it. This book follows Ashbee's observation through to its ultimate realization in the Garden City Movement, early council housing, and a new form of urban life.

The story told here is an almost exclusively English one as I am acutely aware that Northern Ireland, Wales, and especially Scotland, have their own versions of this story. I am also aware that I write, for once, not purely as an architectural historian with a professional interest in this subject but passionately as one raised in the lee of the Movement. The happy accident of being the child of itinerant publicans in the West Country ensured I was unwittingly formed by the landscape and buildings of the Cotswolds. Its soft honey-coloured buildings, whose roofs are the same colour as its walls, seemed to have grown from the earth that supports them. Little wonder that the region and its traditions became a touchstone for the Movement. Only after moving away did I realize that not everyone felt as I did about the place they came from and I now recognize how lucky I was. Lucky also to have subsequently spent my early years as an academic working in some of this country's great art colleges where the crafts still flourished. Gradually they became homogenized into larger institutions and their distinctive traditions sublimated. Urbanism continues to challenge us in various ways both here and across the globe, but the values, and sheer beauty, of Arts and Crafts architecture can still give us hope for a better life for all.

# Chapter 1

# Themes and Variations

THIS BOOK IS AN INTRODUCTION TO THE architecture of the Arts and Crafts Movement, one of the most exciting and influential artistic movements the British Isles has ever produced. The name was created by the lawyer turned bookbinder Thomas Cobden-Sanderson (1840–1922) who, in 1883, first coined the phrase 'Arts and Crafts'. Little can he have imagined the influence the seemingly innocent joining together of these two words was to have. Yet the very fact that he, in common with many others, had abandoned a conventional and lucrative career in favour of 'the simple life' sought by pursuing the craft ideal of making beautiful and useful products with his hands that underpins the movement, is compelling evidence

William Morris, the leader of the movement, photographed by Edward Hollyer in 1888. When he died, his close friend Phillip Webb said, 'I feel like I've lost a limb.' (Scanned from J.W. Mackail, *The Life of William Morris*, 1899)

Opposite: Even a door can be a work of art – door handle and key escutcheon in Oxford University Museum.

Front cover illustration by Henry Wilson for the programme of *Beauty's Awakening*. It shows the knight, Trueheart, fighting with the dragon, Aschemon, over the sleeping Spirit of Beauty. (Author's collection)

of that influence. Many people have heard of the Arts and Crafts Movement – most likely because of William Morris (1834–96) and his wallpaper designs. Some may even be aware of his famous saying, 'Have nothing in your houses that you do not know to be useful, or believe to be beautiful.'[1] The fact that he considered such a warning necessary was because in Victorian England the arts generally were in a state of turmoil as a new style for the century was sought.

## Beauty's Awakening

*Beauty's Awakening*, this book's subtitle, refers to a type of fairy-story – a masque that was an elaborate and spectacular form of play with music. A mixture of *Sleeping Beauty, Beauty and the Beast* and similar stories, it was performed by members of the Art Workers' Guild in 1899 in London. This guild is arguably the key organization of the Arts and Crafts Movement. Founded in 1884, the vast majority of architects and craftsmen discussed in this book were at one time or another members of it and membership is at least one convenient way of defining the movement. Like the medieval guilds it based itself on, it was a form of secret society of like-minded individuals – part trade union, part freemasonry – who shared an interest in reviving the crafts that were dying out in industrial Britain. First noticed in the 1880s, the movement grew to prominence in the 1890s and succeeded in exerting its influence well into the 1920s and even the 1930s. Opposed to the idea of the arts being about style, they created a new approach based upon regenerating society.

## 'We want no style. . .'

The Society for the Protection of Ancient Buildings, one of the world's first conservation bodies and a key organization of the Arts and Crafts Movement, put this issue of style well in its Manifesto of 1877 claiming that, '. . . the civilized world of the nineteenth

John Ruskin, the chief intellectual guide for the movement, painted in a vivid Pre-Raphaelite manner by John Everett Millais. (© Ashmolean Museum, University of Oxford)

century has no style of its own amidst its wide knowledge of the styles of other centuries.'[2]. For many, the burning issue of the day was what was this style to be?

However, the critic John Ruskin (1819–1900), the originator of so many Arts and Crafts ideals, argued against the whole idea of pursuing a style as the basis of architecture. 'We want no style,' he wrote, '. . . it does not matter one marble splinter whether we have an old or a new architecture, but it matters everything whether we have an architecture truly so called or not.'[3] The architect E.S. Prior (1857–1932) was even more adamant: 'Surely no style can help us,' he wrote.[4] To such men the search seemed pointless. Looking back shortly after the century ended, and to the succession of revivalist styles, another member of the movement, the architect Reginald Blomfield (1856–1942), lamented that, 'Modern architecture seems incapable of progress except in a circle.'[5]

The Egyptian House, Penzance, demonstrates the extent of the British Empire and the wealth of styles available to copy.

The grand staircase of the Foreign Office by George Gilbert Scott. The key building in the 'Battle of the Styles', its Italianate appearance was a long way from his preferred Gothic. (Open Government Licence version 1.0, courtesy HM Foreign Office)

## An age of revivals

Architecture had reached the point that the only way it was thought of was as historicist, in other words copying the architecture of the past in an archaeologically accurate way. Archaeology, a relatively new discipline, was regularly accused of creating the conditions for revivalism by its desire to accurately record the remains of the past. The conflict, principally between the supporters of the Gothic Revival and those who favoured various forms of Classicism, came to the fore over the design of the new Foreign Office. George Gilbert Scott (1811–78) won in a Gothic Revival style – not dissimilar to the fantasy palace of railway hotels at St Pancras he built later – but the government, in the shape of Lord Palmerston, wanted Classical. Government won but not until a heated debate lasting many years gave the profession a bloody nose. We can perhaps get an insight into what it was like by reading the recollections of Charles Voysey (1857–1941), ironically the architect most associated in the public imagination with a recognizable Arts and Crafts 'style'. Describing the average nineteenth-century architect, he recalled: 'When a client called for a design the first questions asked were: What style do you want? Next: What period of that particular style? Given the style and the period, books were drawn from the library shelves and approved examples of details were chosen; a chimneypiece or chimney, an oriel, a door, or a window from several books. Such things as these were copied and welded together and like the ingredients of a Christmas pudding equally hard to digest.'[6]

Accordingly, typical Victorian architecture might look Egyptian, medieval, Elizabethan, Italian, Greek, Spanish and so on but never modern, of its own age. Certain architects specialized in certain styles from the past; others were adept at moving from one to another without any sense of a style as something personal. Even architects who were supporters of the aims of the Arts and Crafts Movement, such as T.G.

The attractive gable end of Trinity College, Oxford, designed by T.G. Jackson. Looking every inch an old Jacobean building it was actually completed in 1885.

Situated in leafy Kensington, Webb's London house for George Howard, the 9th Earl of Carlisle, and a great patron of the movement, was attacked for not conforming to a recognizable style. (CC BY-SA 3.0)

Jackson (1835–1924), built a career out of reviving past styles such as the Elizabethan and Jacobean.

Little wonder then that when Philip Webb (1831–1915) was designing No.1 Palace Gate, Kensington, for his wealthy patron George Howard (1843–1911), the 9th Earl of Carlisle, its design proved to be controversial as it was on Crown land and required special permission. Sir James Pennethorne (1801–71), the Crown's advisor, sought advice from experts and was exasperated to find that none of them could tell what style the building was designed in! For Webb, the most important architect of the movement, that was a measure of success, and reminds us that our idea of originality is a very modern idea that would have not troubled most of our Victorian and Edwardian predecessors.

So it is important to state right at the start that the

Arts and Crafts Movement, at its best, was not a style like others of the day, based on an archaeologically accurate understanding of their forms and decorative details and then copying them for modern buildings, but an approach, a collection of radical, progressive, utopian ideals that its followers – disciples even – adhered to.

## In search of tradition . . . the timeless way of building

If these architects weren't copying the famous styles of the past, how were they thinking of architecture? As a broadly based movement there was no agreed philosophy and no common document or manifesto that sets out its approach. Rather these ideals were

Photograph of cottages at Chedworth, Gloucestershire taken from *Old Cottages, Farm-houses, and other Stone Buildings in the Cotswold District* by W. Galsworthy Davie and E. Guy Dawber, published in 1905 by Batsford. Batsford were one of the new wave of publishers successfully exploiting the use of photography to popularize traditional architecture such as these attractive cottages.

concerned with creating a more humane, functional, simple, satisfying, and beautiful architecture based on examples found in the countryside built out of traditional materials by traditional methods. It was idealistic in seeing this as a way of combating the worst excesses of modern urban life in Victorian Britain, and maybe solving them by looking to a seemingly timeless vernacular architecture created by skilled local craftsmen – not professional architects.

The critic Lawrence Weaver (1876–1930), describing Ernest Gimson's Stoneywell Cottage, said of it that it was 'Roughly, even rudely, built... no tool has been lifted to mark a false impression of age. If it has the air of being old, it is only because old ways have been followed not because the least effort has been made to impart a false air of antiquity.'[7] When a local returned to the area after many years away he was confused, as he didn't remember the building – it looked as if it had always been there. This was a further measure of success for an Arts and Crafts Movement architect. M.H. Baillie Scott (1865–1945) was another of the architects who designed '. . . in

different places traditional houses and cottages which could not be distinguished externally from those that had been in the district for centuries.'[8] Imbued with a deep sense of Romanticism he wrote that, 'A man should make his own dwelling as the birds of the air, their nests.'[9] As a sentiment this is not far from John Keats' claims for Romantic poetry that, '. . . if it doesn't come as naturally as the leaves on the trees it had better not come at all.'

## The use of traditional building typology

In their determination to avoid historicism (or revivalism as it was also called) the architects of the Arts and Crafts Movement instead worked with a series of archetypes; that is building forms that were not, like style, subject to the vagaries of fashion. Instead of Classical or Gothic, Byzantine or Baroque styles, they thought rather of the cottage, the long house, the farmhouse, the manor house, the castle, the quad

Great Coxwell tithe barn – this building symbolized everything that was right about medieval architecture for Morris, who compared it to a great cathedral.

or cloister, and above all the barn. Morris, after he had moved into an old manor house at Kelmscott in Gloucestershire, was fond of taking visitors to see the former monastic barn at Great Coxwell and wrote of it as, '. . . the finest piece of architecture in England . . . unapproachable in its dignity, as beautiful as a cathedral, yet with no ostentation of the builder's art'. J.D. Sedding (1838–91) also acknowledged this approach in a lecture he gave at the Whitechapel Guild of Crafts in 1890, arguing that they all '. . . had the same kind of windows and doors, roofs and buttresses . . . the same vein of humour is tapped for secular or religious structure.'[10] Within most of these typologies lay the traditional open hall house, a hark back to a communal way of living where a whole community would eat together in a large open space below an enormous sheltering roof warmed by a central fire. It is one of the oldest and the most essential of communal structures and found its way into a wide variety of Arts and Crafts buildings from the country house, the church, and the early twentieth-century council house.

Fig. 7. House at Scrivelsby, Lincolnshire. The roof rests directly on the ground and the ridge-tree is carried by pairs of inclined straight principals or crucks, two in each gable.

Teapot Hall, Scrivelsby, Lincolnshire. An illustration from C.F. Innocent's *The Development of English Building Construction*. Published in 1916, despite its bland title, the book was a bible of traditional building materials and techniques aimed at helping young architects pass their exams. Teapot Hall became an instantly recognizable image of timeless building techniques for the next twenty years or more until it was lost to fire.

The image of shelter it epitomized was an important reference back to the origins of building – thereby validating Arts and Crafts architecture – and was symbolized in its most primitive state by the building known as Teapot Hall. Equally psychologically important for the sense of safety and protection it gave was another archetype used with some regularity, the courtyard, or quad – a harkening back to collegiate living which appears in buildings such as Waterlow Court by Baillie Scott in Hampstead Garden Suburb.

By studying the past in terms of these building types, rather than famous styles and their systems of ornament and decoration, the movement avoided the charge of being historicist, of perpetuating the 'Battle of the Styles'. The architect Norman Jewson (1884–1975) expressed it well, writing that, 'My own buildings I wanted to have the basic qualities of the best houses of their locality, built in the local traditional way in the local materials, but not copying the details which properly belonged to the period in which they were built.'[11]

## Escapism with a purpose

In many respects the Arts and Crafts were but a part of the larger Romantic Movement and its view of nature as a 'cure' for modern life. It was escapist, but this was escapism with a purpose, imbued with a moral crusade to make life better. We need to remember that despite his subsequent reputation as the movement's leader, and as an important designer in his own right, Morris was best known in his own lifetime as a poet writing modern folklore stories based on Chaucer and Scandinavian sagas. In the prologue to his epic poem *The Earthly Paradise* (1868–70) he unwittingly announced the movement's poetic and artistic ideals with the invitation to:

> Forget six counties overhung with smoke,
> Forget the snorting steam and piston stroke,
> Forget the spreading of the hideous town;
> Think rather of the pack-horse on the down,
> And dream of London, small and white and clean,
> The clear Thames bordered by its gardens green.

Like the story of *Sleeping Beauty*, Morris and his followers saw it as their duty to open the country's eyes, to awaken their sense of beauty, to the rapidly vanishing countryside as industry overwhelmed it. They saw the traditional building crafts dying out in favour of mass-production, and the craftsman becoming a factory-worker, an extension of the machine. In his most influential book for the development of the movement, *The Stones of Venice* (1851–53), Ruskin, also capable of writing fairy-stories for children, railed against factory production, arguing that, 'Men were not intended to work with the accuracy of tools, to be precise and perfect in all their actions.'[12]

Arnold Mitchell's 'Trevelloe' nestles deep in a wooded clearing in the Lamorna Valley, its giant catslide roofs of local slate sweeping down to almost touch the ground. They must have big cats in Cornwall!

## The architecture of fairyland

So not only is this the architecture of tradition but also of the fairy-story, filled with simple rustic dwellings more than palaces, many of its buildings being described as like Hansel and Gretel houses. It is one of the many ways in which the movement idealized the countryside and pre-industrial life to seem almost magical. The Prussian commentator, Hermann Muthesius (1861–1927), whose book *Das Englische Haus* is one of the best guides to the movement's architecture, saw many of the buildings as having '. . . stepped into the world of fantasy'. Another contemporary writer, thinking of the architecture of Voysey, wrote that:

When I was a child I was excited by fairy-tale houses having enormous roofs and practically no windows, by doorways to Wonderland having arches so low that an ordinary person would need to eat one of Alice's reducing cakes in order to pass under them, by tables whose legs not only went down to the floor but sprouted upwards toward the ceiling, by patterns made

of cockyolly birds inspecting with surprise square trees slightly smaller than themselves.[13]

And May Morris (1862–1938), William Morris's youngest daughter, wrote of Melsetter House, designed by W.R. Lethaby (1857–1931), on the Isle of Hoy, as seeming '. . . like the embodiment of some of those fairy palaces of which my father wrote.'[14]

## Politics and the Movement

That the movement was not escapist is ably demonstrated by its political stance. Socialism, and left-leaning politics generally, was then a new political position and informed much of the movement's work. The posters and banners designed by Walter Crane (1845–1915) in support of radical politics shared in the fairy-tale imagery of Arthur Rackham and others. Both Morris and Webb, very much the founders of the movement, were devoted to the cause of socialism. When on holiday in Italy, Webb complained to a friend that his copies of the socialist weekly *The Commonweal* hadn't been received. And in his first public lecture in 1877 Morris famously declared, 'I do not want art for a few, any more than education for a few, or freedom for a few.' Neither was he afraid to bite the hand that fed him, Lethaby recording that:

Sir Lowthian Bell told Mr Alfred Powell that one day he heard Morris talking and walking about in an excited way [in Webb's Rounton Grange], and went to inquire if anything was wrong. He turned on me like a mad animal – 'It is only that I spend my life ministering to the swinish luxury of the rich.'[15]

This outburst is regularly used as evidence to castigate Morris in particular, and the movement in general, as being hypocritical in designing houses and objects for the rich that the working classes couldn't possibly afford. Rather, I would argue, it should be taken as evidence of his frustration at the state of society that restricted their products to those who

Walter Crane's 'A Garland for May Day' illustrated the front cover of the socialist magazine *The Clarion*. (Author's collection)

Voysey placed individualism over collectivism. And if support for female emancipation and the Suffragettes were taken as evidence of left-wing politics then many fell foul of its claims. Arnold Mitchell (1863–1944) was one of many who opposed the RIBA allowing women to become members of the architectural profession. Not until Ethel Charles (1871–1962) was admitted to the RIBA in 1898 do we find a female architect. Other areas of the building crafts, such as wood carving, or embroidery, were considered more 'appropriate' for women even within the left-leaning politics of the Arts and Crafts Movement. Perhaps the movement was but a staging post on the road towards a craft-based society of equals rather than the solution to the problems created by industry they hoped for.

## Architects and/or craftsmen?

Despite these inequalities one of the most noticeable features of the movement is that it was so broadly based whilst remaining centred on architecture. Although Morris abandoned his career as an architect after eight months he argued that, '. . . the existence of the other arts is bound up with that of Architecture'.[17] It ranged across a variety of media from architecture to textiles, plasterwork to pottery, furniture to glass, ironwork to printing. Neither were these individual crafts practised in isolation by one person; each reaching a peak of perfection in their chosen specialist field. Ernest Gimson (1864–1919) – one of the most talented members of the movement – trained as an architect but is equally, if not better, known for his furniture, plasterwork, and metalwork.

## Amateur or professional?

could afford them. Idealistic, perhaps unrealistic, but Morris and his followers were sincere in their beliefs – and they hung on for some time. As the future poet laureate, John Betjeman (1906–84), when an assistant editor on *The Architectural Review*, recalled of the 1930s, 'To be left was to be sincere. To be right was to be insincere. I think I believed this myself. We were sent thumbing through the early numbers of *The Studio* in search of our heritage of sincerity and socialism in the Arts and Crafts movement of 1890 onwards.'[16] Richard Norman Shaw (1831–1912) had to reassure the parents of one of his pupils that although his chief assistant, Lethaby, was indeed a socialist, he was a socialist '. . . of the gentlest kind'.

Yet not all members of the Arts and Crafts community were on the left politically. Edward Prior, another of Shaw's pupils, certainly was not and neither were some of the next, third generation of Arts and Crafts architects such as Voysey and Baillie Scott. Whilst good-quality state housing after the First World War may be seen as the ultimate realization of Morris's beliefs, Baillie Scott railed against it and both he and

Such dexterity has left the movement open to the charge of amateurism – that they were dabblers rather than real craftsmen and often employed others to execute their designs rather than realizing them with their own hands. In many respects they would have been happy to accept the amateur label, of being 'Jacks-of-all-trades' but masters of none. Sedding argued, 'There is hope in honest error, none in the perfections of the icy stylist.'[18] Increasingly this view became something of a rallying cry in defence of the handicrafts. Yet at the same time as the movement was gaining force the sociologist Thorstein Veblen, in a now highly regarded study, *The Theory of the Leisure Class: An Economic Study of Institutions*, published in 1899, stated the opposing view claiming that:

> ... the visible imperfections of the hand-wrought goods, being honorific, are accounted marks of superiority in point of beauty, or serviceability, or both. Hence has arisen that exaltation of the defective, of which Ruskin and Morris were such eager spokesmen in their time; and on this ground their propaganda of crudity and wasted effort has been taken up and carried forward since their time.

## A profession or an art?

At the time of its creation, architecture was becoming more technically demanding than ever before, also more professional as it responded to new ways of working and sizes and complexity of building. Accordingly, it was also in search of legal control of its membership to exclude the incompetent. However, this was also seen by many as excluding the more artistically inclined, the more experimental, and the more idealistic. In brief, architecture was becoming big business. As T.G. Jackson wrote in 1892 at the peak of the bitter debate over the issue, 'Legislation has at last reached the domain of Art, and it has been seriously proposed to charge Parliament with the duty of providing the public with good architecture and properly qualified architects.'[19]

## A new kind of architect is born

In response to this increasing professionalization, and much else besides, the Arts and Crafts Movement created a new kind of architect, perhaps of a kind that shouldn't even be called architect in the modern sense of the word. Norman Jewson, an assistant to Gimson in their rural Gloucestershire workshop in Sapperton, wrote that:

> The professional side of architecture had never appealed to me. I was aware that it was generally considered to be impossible to become a successful architect without living in a town, spending much of one's time making social contacts whilst most of the actual work was done by one's office staff, but for me it was architecture I was interested in, not making a large income as an architect.

Architecture, of the sort that Jewson described, was becoming a commercial undertaking rather than the hobby of 'gentlemen-architects', or part of a 'living-tradition' of vernacular building, and so seemed to demand that it became more professional to inspire confidence in its clients.

These clients were also changing to be companies, institutions and large public bodies, not aristocratic wealthy patrons. A successful professional architect, such as George Gilbert Scott, the architect best known for the Midland Hotel, St Pancras, and the Albert Memorial (amongst over 800 other buildings) and at the centre of the so-called 'Battle of the Styles', enjoyed a lucrative career during which at any one time his office employed in excess of 'thirty draughtsmen in a back office'.[20] For the movement, the fear was that this was the start of the total industrialization of the building process where artistically inclined architects were pushed out in favour of an easy repetitive architecture based on commerce, not art. In deliberate contrast, Arts and Crafts architects prided themselves on having small offices with very few assistants so they could be involved in every detail of the job. It is perhaps no accident that such a practice emerged in the same century that Karl Marx was identifying the bad effects of this increasing division of labour, of specialization, as resulting in workers' alienation from society.

George Gilbert Scott's St Pancras railway hotel. One of the greatest buildings of the Gothic Revival, this grand medieval palace of a railway station hotel gives an idea of what Scott's Foreign Office buildings might have been like had the prime minister of the day liked Gothic architecture. (© User: Colin/Wikimedia Commons/CC BY-SA 3.0)

## Back to nature

At the heart of the movement's aesthetics lay a love of nature, the countryside, traditional craft skills, and a turning away from the ills of industrialization that were visibly destroying beauty before its very eyes. Gimson, when asked in a Manchester tea room what he wanted, replied, 'Something made in the country please.' Possibly just down the road from him in Manchester, one of its most famous architects, Edgar Wood (1860–1935), was arguing, 'Nature in some form or other must of necessity have been the original source of all design.'[21]

## The example of the medieval guild

In many ways the architects of the Arts and Crafts Movement would view a book on its buildings with dismay, because it runs the risk of isolating them from the other 'arts connected to building' as they saw it. Architecture should be a collaborative, integrated occupation between craftsmen, under the direction – not dictatorship – of an experienced master. This, they believed, was how pre-industrial buildings – both great and small – were built. They argued that medieval buildings in particular were built by men working in guilds that regulated their working conditions fairly, who were trained by a master, and under a system that allowed individual freedom of expression. This freedom, they argued, could be seen in the beauty and variety of carving in a cathedral. It was a Romantic idea fostered of a fascination with the medieval Gothic world fed by writers such as Sir Walter Scott, and poets such as Shelley, Keats, and most of all the Arthurian romances of Tennyson.

## St Edward the Confessor, Kempley

A little-known building that exemplifies many of the character traits of the Arts and Crafts Movement is St Edward the Confessor, Kempley, in Gloucestershire. Built with local materials in a traditional way, using local builders under the direction of experienced travelling masons, it deserves to be better known. Designed as a chapel of ease for the nearby twelfth-century church, its architect was Albert Randall Wells (1877–1942). No plans survive and it seems that Wells evolved the unusual design with his workmen as building progressed. He had recently acted as Lethaby's clerk of works at All Saints' Church in Brockhampton. Built just across the border in Herefordshire, All Saints' was completed in 1902 and Wells brought much of what he had learnt on that job with him to Kempley. Trained in Hastings by his father, Arthur Wells, he was one of those architects called 'Wandering Architects' by Michael Drury in his book of the same name. Detmar Blow (1867–1939) was another example. These were the architects who believed in working out the design of a building more or less on site with their fellow craftsmen, adapting to local conditions, employing local craftsmen, materials and traditions so that the building was as grounded in the locality as it could be.

It seems Wells received the commission as a result of his brother, Linley Wells, knowing the client, William Lygon, the 7th Earl Beauchamp. The Earl had recently returned from being Governor of New South Wales and had already begun the building of the church, so Randall Wells inherited a building with some foundations already laid out. Beauchamp, the inheritor of nearby Madresfield Court, requested that the church be filled with light from the west, not the east end as was usual. This gives the building an unusual, and somewhat innovative, quality at the east end where the altar is cloaked in darkness, the west end lit magnificently

by an enormous stone lattice window. This seems to be an enlarged version of one of the windows Wells had constructed for Lethaby at Brockhampton. Apart from the well-lit west end the client also requested that the building's eaves should be kept low. They are. So low as to feel as if they scrape the ground to the rear elevation. Here the church has an agricultural feel in its simplicity: short, sturdy buttresses supporting the equally stocky-looking rubble wall.

For the basic structure, Wells brought to Kempley not only his experience at Brockhampton but some of the same team of masons who had worked with him, supplementing them with local labour and employing a local builder as foreman, a Mr R. James. The stone came from only seven miles away in the Forest of Dean and the oak was supplied from the nearby Beauchamp estate. The roof (now changed) was originally covered with stone tiles quarried and dressed by the workmen from a piece of land procured especially for the purpose in the Forest of Dean – a practice which had dried out in the district shortly before this. Thin slabs of stone are revealed internally in window splays to show how the building is constructed. The enormous scissor beams of the roof truss at the east end support a series of carved figures. The edges of the beam they sit on was simply ornamented by the village carpenters using their draw-knives and chisels whilst the decoration to the face of the beams was carved out and gouged by Randall and his brother Linley. It was then painted by the village painters with a thin coat of ivory black, grounded in white,

St Edward the Confessor, Kempley. Agricultural forms and early Christianity combined to create a hymn of praise to local materials and building traditions.

The largely windowless south wall in particular has an agricultural feel in its strength and simplicity, with short, sturdy buttresses blending seamlessly into the rest of the fabric.

The size of the large lattice window to the west end is an inventively powerful enlargement of a similar window in Lethaby's church at nearby Brockhampton.

The simple carving and decoration of the rood beam was carried out by Randall Wells and his brother, working alongside the local village craftsmen.

The construction is honestly expressed by the architect here – the large wooden cruck wilfully bisecting the chancel window, the stone of the window jambs fanning out at the top with no attempt to disguise the individual stones.

The primitive stone font, designed and carved by Wells, continues the simplicity of the church's decoration with two bands of folk carving representing the baptismal water.

The extraordinary triangular tracery of the west end window seen close up, glazed with old Dutch hand-made glass, and with sheep's-tail window catches and stays made by the local village blacksmith.

Delicate mother-of-pearl inlay enlivens the chancel candlestick and other pieces of woodwork supplied by the Sapperton workshops.

The roof trusses reveal both honesty in materials and construction – you can see what they are made of and how they are held together. Beyond them in the noumenal light of the east end can be glimpsed the rood beam and its figures.

and filled with the deep vibrant colours which lurk within the darkness of the east end.

For the more decorative aspects of the church, Wells worked alongside fellow craftsmen. Above the entrance is a relief figure of Christ the Peacemaker carved by Wells himself. Wells also carved the impressively primitive font which, together with the dedication to St Edward the Confessor, serves to heighten the impression of an Early Christian church without recourse to an Early Christian style. Internally the enormous west window is fitted with wrought-iron casements, fitted with old Dutch glass and ironwork supplied by the village blacksmith, Jack Smallman. Leading Arts and Crafts figures from the Sapperton workshops in Gloucestershire supplied furniture including the iron candlesticks and candelabra by Gimson, and the lectern with inlaid mother-of-pearl by Ernest Barnsley (1863–1926). The rood figures are vigorously carved in pine by David Gibb, thought to be one of the last ships' figure-head carpenters left in the country. His muscular vernacular depiction of Christ, supported by figures of St Mary and St John, was too much for the diocese and Wells recorded that initially, 'The Bishops had them pulled down but they have since been replaced.'

## By rule of thumb

What is so persuasive about this building is its simplicity. Stripped of its more religious ornament, it could be an agricultural building. Architecture is a remote art, where building isn't. Morris gave up architecture because he couldn't get involved in it enough, his temperament needed to be immersed rather than distant as it is in architecture. In the nineteenth century the architect was increasingly becoming someone who simply drew up the plans for someone else to build from – and often the all-important details were later changed so that the architect's intentions weren't fully realized. Morris would have surely liked the process that built the church at Kempley. As the writer Randal Phillips put it in *The Modern English House*, 'The old timber houses were not first drawn on paper with ruler and compass. They were built by rule of thumb, the timbers being used just as they came to hand.'[22]

Sedding, who but for his early death in 1891 could have exerted a much greater influence on the movement, put it most directly: 'The real architect of a building must be his own clerk of works, his own carver, his own director, he must be the familiar spirit of the structure as it rises from the ground . . . to make the most of the site and the building as applied to it.'[23] This is exactly what Wells managed at Kempley and what makes it such a good example.

## From art to society

As a consequence of the remoteness of the architect from the rest of the building team, there was also a strong feeling amongst architects associated with the movement that the class differences between architects and builders, between professionals and tradesmen, was such that it was hard to work collaboratively on a building as the two were increasingly kept apart by the system of general contracting – in fact the two need never meet. The method of working adopted by Wells – by what was called direct labour in contrast to general contracting – was urged by Ruskin and others, not merely for the creation of beautiful works of art but could, and should, be applied to society at large to close this class divide. It was seen as an antidote to the economic system that had created the method of fixed-price general contracting brought about by the General Contractor in the seventeenth century. This was a system whereby middlemen, such as Nicholas Barbon (1640–98) in London, undertook to put up buildings for a fixed sum and then made profit by sub-contracting to individual craftsmen or groups of craftsmen working outside the increasingly attacked protection afforded by the guild system. Many such contractors established their own large contracting firms, eroding working conditions for craftsmen, undermining the trade guilds, and relied on standardized pattern books for supplying designs rather than employing architects.

Influential figures such as Arthur Heygate Mackmurdo (1851–1942), creator of the Century Guild, and Arthur Penty (1875–1937), an architect and promoter of Guild Socialism, hoped for the creation of a fairer society if a medieval guild system could be recreated in Victorian Britain and thereby restore the power of the guilds, and raise the standard of craftsmanship and quality of life for the craftsmen. C.R. Ashbee, more than any other, attempted this by taking the Guild and School of Handicraft he established in the East End of London in 1888 to the Cotswold village of Chipping Camden in 1902.

## Is it an Arts and Crafts building?

It follows that, maddeningly, as Arts and Crafts is a set of ideas and not a style, the products of the Arts and Crafts Movement are not necessarily easily recognizable. They have few visual characteristics in common and so do not display a particular visual similarity. This is one of the very confusing aspects of the movement. So much, and of such visual disparity, seems to be called Arts and Crafts today that it is hard to understand what it is. Perhaps it is better to ask questions such as 'how was it designed?' On paper down to the last detail so the job could be priced by rival building contractors, or by a series of rough sketches so details could be left to the workmen on the site to supply their own creativity? Did the architect command a large office of assistants he could use as clerks of works to ensure his drawings were carried out to the letter or did he visit the site frequently himself, working closely with one of his assistants as a prized and trusted colleague? Is the architect's name acknowledged prominently in all the publicity about the building or does he appear at the end of a long list of named builders and craftsmen who contributed to the work? Were the materials the best of their kind and imported a considerable distance at great expense or local, reflecting the regional geology of the area? Did the construction take advantage of the most advanced new methods of building or continue the traditional way of building with the local materials in the area? Was the decoration a learned reflection of historic ornament or inspired by the local flora and fauna? Was the site levelled before work started to make construction easier or was its topography, existing buildings, viewpoints and vegetation noticed and incorporated into the design?

## Innovation within tradition

If the movement was not concerned to be working out a recognizable new style it was also not concerned to be slavishly copying the styles of the past. Therefore, there was an implicit, if not explicit, recognition that the Arts and Crafts ideals, if followed, would produce a new kind of architecture where, as Lethaby put it, beauty would come in '. . . as a sort of by-product'. Pre-industrial techniques were studied as a means of creating new buildings and then the visual result,

the appearance or look of the building, was a consequence of the process, they argued. Lethaby and others claimed that style needed to be forgotten in favour of construction. He wrote:

> We cannot forget our historical knowledge nor would we if we might. The important question is, can it be organized or must we continue to be betrayed by it? The only agreement that seems possible is agreement on a scientific basis, on an endeavour after perfect structural efficiency. If we could agree on this we need not trouble about beauty for that would take care of itself.[24]

The distaste for the pursuit of style as an end in itself is also well expressed by his dismissal of twentieth-century Modernism as '. . . only another design humbug to pass off with a shrug – ye olde modernist style – we must have a style to copy – what funny stuff this art is.'[25]

This pursuit of 'perfect structural efficiency' allowed for considerable innovation and increasingly began to embrace more modern, industrial materials and methods such as concrete and steel. A seemingly revivalist building, like the new Westminster Cathedral, could be greatly admired for its construction, its shallow concrete saucer domes not hidden beneath a secondary dome as Sir Christopher Wren had done at St Paul's Cathedral – that was an architecture of constructional deception, not 'perfect structural efficiency'. Both Webb, and his disciple Lethaby, greatly admired Bentley's work at Westminster but admired its construction most of all before its iron, brick and concrete was covered in decoration.

## A warning: Arts and Crafts is not Art Nouveau

Similarly, modern materials lay at the heart of Art Nouveau, which exploited them for daring decorative effect. However, Art Nouveau, as it so often is, should never be confused with Arts and Crafts. All that links them is a regard for nature and a determination not to copy the past in a slavish manner. A highly decorative style, associated primarily with mainland Europe, and Scotland especially in the person of Charles Rennie Mackintosh, it was viewed with dismay by most members of the Arts and Crafts Movement. Walter Crane, in his 1892 book *The Claims of Decorative Art*, attacked it as 'a strange decorative disease', whilst Blomfield referred to '... the portentous aberrations of *L'Art Nouveau*', seeing in it '... ornament for the sake of ornament, to carve and paint for the sake of doing it without contributing to the total effect of a building'.[26] And he sustained his attack throughout the book, concluding that, 'I need not say more about Art Nouveau except to warn you to be on your guard against these futile attempts at originality.' And they were not alone. To be caught practising what was derogatively referred to as 'the squirm' as a student at the Central School of Art and Craft (the first local authority art college in the country) was to risk censure if not expulsion, so vehemently was it opposed by the constellation of the Arts and Crafts Movement who taught there.

## Conclusion

In the story that follows, the movement is traced from its roots in the writings of Ruskin, the Gothic Revival, the Pre-Raphaelites, and its key architect, Philip Webb, to the foundation of organizations such as SPAB, the Art Workers' Guild, the Arts and Crafts Exhibition Society, and the protest against the RIBA by the Memorialists. Out of this emerged the second generation – the sons of Shaw – especially its most creative members Lethaby and Prior, followed by the third generation of Voysey, Baillie Scott and Lutyens. The penultimate chapter looks at other architects who came to prominence in the major provincial cities, before concluding with the high point – the Garden City Movement. Each chapter is followed by an in-depth look at a representative building that is open to the public. In the hopes this book will whet your appetite, a list of further buildings to visit, and even those you can stay in, is included at the end with suggestions of other books to read.

Oxford University Museum. Built to bring natural science teaching together at the university.

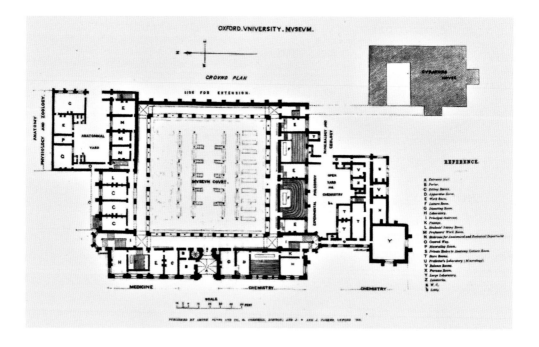

Although William Morris is the name most well known in relation to the Arts and Crafts Movement, he owes a great intellectual debt to John Ruskin. Ruskin was very much a presence in Oxford when Morris arrived as an undergraduate at Exeter College in 1852 and commanded a powerful position as one of the leading critics of the day. One of Ruskin's many activities was his involvement in the realization of the Oxford University Museum.

When, via his old friend Henry Acland, he heard that the architectural competition for the building had been won by the Irish firm of Deane and Woodward he was overjoyed. He knew this actually meant another friend, the architect Benjamin Woodward, had won. All three men – Acland, Ruskin and Woodward – had studied together at Christ Church College, Oxford. Ruskin wrote back to Acland:

> . . . I have just received your telegraphic message from Woodward, and am going to thank God for it, and lie down to sleep... To me this is a kind of first fruits for sowing of which 'I knew not whether I should prosper'. I am glad after all that it is at Oxford.[27]

Ruskin's excitement – evidently shared by Woodward to the extent that he had sent a telegraph to Acland to let him know he'd won the competition out of thirty-two entrants – was due to Woodward

sharing so many of Ruskin's ideas about the nature of architecture. The competition was won in 1851; work began in 1855 and was opened (still unfinished as it is today) in 1860. Although the university voted a considerable sum of money for its construction, much of its decoration, including the carved stone capitals, had to be paid for by public donation.

Externally at first sight the museum resembles a large medieval building such as a cloth hall, or a monastic guest house. A central entrance tower bisects two equal ranges of two storeys with the slate roof patterned with counterpointing rows of unusual triangular dormer windows. The walls are constructed of smooth local limestone, cut finely by the masons to

be what is known as ashlar – that's to say not rough and rubbly, but smooth, almost polished, and so revealing the skill of the mason even before we get to consider the finer carved work of the decorative carver. And here is where even greater skill, and a story, is revealed.

As the building was to house the university's collections of natural history and geology and provide a teaching base for the natural sciences at Oxford, Woodward's design reflects this in all the carving. In so doing it reflects Ruskin's attitude towards religion and the natural world. Ruskin was not alone at the time in seeing the natural world as a 'second bible' where God's purpose was revealed. Accordingly even though the

A detail of the roof showing how its architect played with simple geometrical shapes in imitation of geological forms – and note the two different colours of slate to imply strata.

The low-relief carving to the entrance contrasts with the natural forms of a briar rose with a geological bed, also suggestive of Romanesque architectural decoration..

Is this where the money ran out? Two Gothic Revival window openings on the front of the museum – one finished, the other not.

overall form of the building is medieval, and its more precise character is Gothic – and Gothic of the then favoured thirteenth century – its decoration is not medieval at all but modern, naturalistic, an attempt to 'hold a mirror up to nature' as the Romantic poets had done at the start of the century. Here you will find no carvings of angels, no saints, no crucifix, but plants and animals. It is not a sacred building but a secular one – and yet it is sacred in seeing nature as a second bible revealing God's creation. As one enters, the low relief carving to the left and right contains figures and animals linked by a sinuous briar rose, creepers and vines. Above this is a dense layer of repetitive abstract carving – not quite roll-billet (a form of Romanesque decoration) as there's so much of it – more of a geological bed – but not without the suggestion of the Romanesque, of Early Christianity. And this is a building full of suggestion but also embedded in the religious debates

within science and religion of the day.

The preference for thirteenth-century Gothic is not restricted to the main entrance but carried through into the window openings spread across the beautifully ashlared front – a combination of coupled lancets to the ground floor and more ornate plate tracery windows to the first floor, all, or nearly all, with naturalistic carvings of plant forms to the mouldings, sometimes containing animals, sometimes not. The inconsistency seems odd. Here and there hard squared-off blocks of stone project from the wall surface almost as if some of the windows have been left unfinished. And so they have. The story this façade tells is one not only of God's creation, but of man's fallibility. Put simply, the money ran out. Carving of this quality was expensive and carvers of this ability were hard to find. Woodward brought with

him a family of stone masons, the O'Sheas, who demonstrated perfectly Ruskin's ideas about the nature of Gothic.

Sadly the inside is also left unfinished but only the plastering of the exposed brickwork, which was to have received painted murals – medieval battle scenes to the ground floor all topped by another running vine motif. But if the exterior plays with the Gothic tradition in updating its sculptural motifs, the interior simply blows them away. What the restless pattern of triangular dormers and ventilators and polychromatic slate roof hides is a large lightweight internal structure of iron columns and beams, strung together with coils of iron foliage and all supporting a completely transparent internal roof of thick plate glass. There is no external clue to prepare the visitor and the passage from lofty entrance porch to botanic railway station, from dark to light, and

The shock of the new technology – little on the outside prepares the visitor for the spectacular interior. Its system of cast-iron columns and arches allow a glazed roof to let the maximum amount of daylight in. In the evenings, the museum was lit by gas lamps.

Light streams through the heavy plate-glass roof to be filtered through metal palms and onto the cast-iron arches stencilled with medieval patterns.

porch but takes over in the interior. Both the stone floor of the main courts, but particularly the peripheral walkways that reinforce the monastic connotations by recreating the space as cloisters and cloister garth, are patterned by a variety of different flooring materials, laid in a variety of patterns to suggest geological formations. Again triangles dominate – a theme carried through from the roof to the interior. It crops up again in the carving to the wooden architraves, and then again – perhaps unwittingly? – in the pattern created overhead by the overlapping plate glass. Between these two elements – heaven and earth – and the arcades that enclose the space reminiscent of one of Ruskin's favourite buildings, the Doge's Palace in Venice – is a welter of more cultured triangular forms – the pointed arches of the cast-iron structure.

To the side walls of brick and stone, a similar pattern of openings to what we saw on the exterior is repeated. Paired arches to the ground floor, larger groups of arches to the upper. Combine this ascending admittance of light with the glass roof of the courts and clearly, very clearly, this externally heavy, rather lumpen building gets lighter as the internal volume grows and the light is filtered by cast-iron fronds, palm leaves, and exotic plants from around the world. Here and there convention breaks out – each iron column

from ignorance to revelation, is simply breathtaking.

Woodward had served his articles with a civil engineer and this may account for his virtuoso display of technical skills in designing for

the new materials of cast iron and glass. One of the many ways in which Ruskin viewed architecture was in its relationship with its materials, with stone, and therefore with geology. This is signalled not only in the bed of billets on the

Slate and stone cut and laid in geologically inspired patterns animates this section of the floor and mirrors similar triangular shapes on the roof and elsewhere.

The angular patterns of the overlapping thick plate-glass contrast with the structures that support them.

The impression of being in a forest is heightened by details of palms and metal leaves woven in and out of conventional Gothic trefoil tracery that form the internal structure.

One of the few conventional capitals – conventional in design only, never were there medieval capitals made out of iron like this. Note the bare brickwork wall behind still waiting to be plastered and painted with medieval murals.

'Look for the bear necessities.' An exhibit seems to rub itself against one of the forest of cast-iron columns.

Every shaft of polished stone in the building is taken from a different part of the British Isles and named to support the educational role of the museum.

One of the delicately carved stone capitals to the museum's arcade – each one is different, often carved from specimens brought in daily by one of the university professors.

begins its journey skywards with a large bell-base typical of thirteenth-century Gothic. As the four shafts – two major, two minor – climb upwards from this base they are held by equally conventional amulets but once they reach the top of their height – the capitals – a great blossoming takes place. Bull-rushes, palms, flowers, all vie with one another for richness. Only one metal capital, treated as an archaeologically accurate rendition of a thirteenth-century capital, can be found amongst the forest of columns, but is so well done it fails to draw attention to itself as anything other than another naturalistic depiction of nature.

Turning to the galleries that encase this 'hothouse' it is apparent that there is a curious and perplexing game of snap being played between stone and metal – what one does, the other echoes. Each marble column of the two stories of arcades has a beautifully carved capital of a botanical specimen; additionally the corbels that support the iron arches are carved with distinct foliage. Turning from these to the courts we see the same, but in iron staring back at us. Looking across the space, the galleries' alternating brown and ochre stone arches are a strong suggestion of Venetian Gothic but despite this foreign reference, overall the building is a hymn of praise to English flora and fauna – Ruskin's favoured Pre-Raphaelite Movement made tangible; his 'first fruits of sowing' may not have created a large harvest but did give an early promise of plenty.

# Chapter 2

# In the Beginning . . .

A chromolithograph of the Crystal Palace from Dickinson's *Comprehensive Pictures of the Great Exhibition of 1851*. Originally mature oak trees were to be felled to make way for the enormous building. In the end it was made large enough to incorporate them and silence local protesters. When he visited, Morris declared it 'ugly'.

## The Great Exhibition of 1851

In 1851 all the industrialized nations of the world were invited to London to display their finest manufactured goods. Assembled under the gigantic glass roof of one of the largest buildings the world had ever seen, and promoted by no lesser figure than Prince Albert (1819–61), this was the Great Exhibition, created to show 'the industry of all nations'.

Opposite: A carefully crafted door catch on one of the pews in All Saints', Selsley, one of the first churches supplied with stained glass by William Morris.

Dedicated to peace, the exhibition had a variety of motives but the reason for this dedication was the fear of revolution. In 1789 the French had overthrown its monarchy in Europe's first bloody revolution. In 1848, only three years before the exhibition, a second wave of revolutions – starting in Sicily then spreading to France, Germany, Italy, and the Austrian Empire – also swept across Europe. All ended in failure, but this didn't allay fear of revolution in Britain. Here, amongst other incidents, there was agitation by the Chartists who planned an enormous mass meeting to take place on Kennington Common on 10 April 1848. The organizers expected a crowd of 200,000, many brought by train from across the country, to deliver a petition to Parliament to demand votes for working-class men. Against this backdrop of revolutions, fears of violence were so strong that the hero of the Napoleonic Wars, the Duke of Wellington, was put in charge of the capital in case of trouble. As it turned out rain dampened spirits and the rally attracted only 20–25,000. Although the exhibition can thus be seen as a counter-revolutionary measure, Britain was concerned not simply to fend off revolution but to improve her balance of payments. The political hope behind the event was that nations which traded together – one of the ultimate aims of the exhibition – would co-operate politically as well as commercially and so peace come to be valued over war.

The unpalatable truth was that despite being seen as the 'workshop of the world', British goods were losing out to foreign competition. A government select committee looked into the reasons for this and concluded that British design was simply not as good as that emanating from France, Italy and Germany. The French, for example, unlike the British, had established a system of architectural and design education based on the Académie in the seventeenth century. Surviving the Revolution, the French were thus far in advance of most of their competitors in encouraging the decorative arts and affording them a status equal to painting and sculpture.

In advance of the Great Exhibition there had been a series of lesser exhibitions promoting what was termed 'art-manufactures'. The brainchild of Henry Cole (1808–82), this involved commissioning leading artists of the day, such as Richard Redgrave (1808–88) and Daniel Maclise (1806–70), to make model, or standardized, designs that united art and industry in their creation. Held at the Society of Arts between 1847 and 1849, Cole's exhibitions were very much forerunners to the Great Exhibition and it was these that brought him to the attention of the exhibition's very active patron, Prince Albert, so that he occupied the key organizational role.

Whilst one part of the exhibition was concerned with 'art-manufactures', elsewhere the impact of mass production, especially examples coming from the United States, demonstrated just how backward Britain (and the rest of Europe) was in terms of industrial design. It needed to learn the lessons of mass production. Machines that could now carve stone ornament and print wallpaper and textiles at the pull of a lever were but the more artistic end of the spectrum. But both Cole's 'art-manufactures' and the examples of mass production came to symbolize everything that was wrong with Britain's approach for the Arts and Crafts Movement as it developed. A young Morris visited and found the whole enterprise ugly. Though well meaning, it encouraged gratuitous ornament for ornament's sake, the reduction of craftsmen to factory workers, and led to the national system of art and design education created after the exhibition – known by the short-hand of the 'South Kensington system' – that encouraged learning by rote rather than developing individual creativity.

## The Crystal Palace

In many respects the building was the epitome of industrialization and stole the show. Covering an area 1,848 by 408 feet, 120 feet wide, and rising over three storeys to reach 72 feet, it was tall enough to allow the enclosure of mature oak trees in Hyde Park. Designed in just eight days by Joseph Paxton (1803–65), and built in a mere nine months, it exploited the new technical possibilities of iron and glass pioneered in the 1830s and 1840s in glasshouses and railway stations. Its walls were of a standard design and herald the beginnings of mass production in architecture. When completed, *Punch* magazine cruelly nick-named the building the 'Crystal Palace'. But the name stuck, more as a term of endearment and wonder than ridicule. *Punch* was not alone in criticizing the 'marvel of the age'. When, in a remarkable demonstration of the benefits of standardized mass-constructed architecture, the building was taken down and re-erected in Sydenham, the influential young art critic John

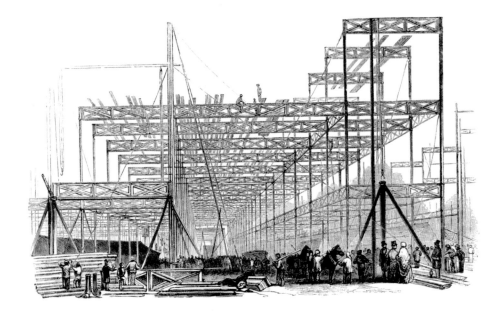

A contemporary illustration of the construction of the Crystal Palace, which was almost as remarkable as its design and ushered in the era of mass-production dreaded by the Arts and Crafts Movement. (*The Crystal Palace* [1851], Peter Berlyn and Charles Fowler [Junior]. Engravings: George Samuel Measom)

Ruskin dismissed it with the words, '. . . in the centre of the nineteenth century, we suppose ourselves to have invented a new style of architecture, when we have magnified a conservatory!'[28] This was, of course, partly true as the architect of the building, Paxton, had made a successful career out of designing greenhouses and conservatories such as the Great Stove at Chatsworth House, completed in 1840.

## John Ruskin and mass-produced architecture

As we've seen in the previous chapter, the search for a 'new style' obsessed many architects and critics in the nineteenth century. Surely this Crystal Palace was the new style of architecture so fervently sought by many? Yet it failed to find favour with Ruskin. His attitude towards the building may be understood if we look more closely at his attitude towards painting.

Ruskin had first come to public attention in 1843

The Great Stove (1836–40) at Chatsworth House, Derbyshire, designed by Joseph Paxton. A modest forerunner of the Crystal Palace, it shows some of the innovative elements such as the zig-zag pattern of the ridge and furrow glazing used later. Larger than any contemporary railway station, Charles Darwin said of it, 'Art beats nature altogether there'.

with the publication of a book entitled *Modern Painters*. Here he argued strongly for painters to reject copying the past – history painting – and seek truth elsewhere. Young artists, he argued, '. . . should go to nature in all singleness of heart, and walk with her laboriously and trustingly, having no other thought but how best to penetrate her meaning; rejecting nothing, selecting nothing, and scorning nothing'.[29] Iron, to Ruskin at least, was not a 'natural material', and so neither was the construction of the Crystal Palace an act of craftsmanship, which he was increasingly concerned with from the time of *The Stones of Venice*. It therefore seems odd that he was so excited by the Oxford University Museum, but as he later wrote '. . . of course it is I – not Acland – who am answerable for it. Woodward was my pupil. I knew from the moment he allowed ironwork, it was all over with the building'.[30]

Ford Madox Brown, *The Last of England* (1855). The artist highlights one of the major issues of the day – the poverty that led many to seek their fortunes elsewhere. (Public domain)

## Ruskin and the Pre-Raphaelite Brotherhood

Eight years after the completion of the University Museum, Ruskin reiterated his advice to young artists concerning the veneration of nature and claimed to have found a group of artists who had put his theory into practice '. . . to the very letter'. This was the Pre-Raphaelite Brotherhood, a group of young artists who put the artistic philosophy of 'truth to nature' before all else. Founded in 1848 by the three painters William Holman Hunt (1827–1910), John Everett Millais (1829–96) and Dante Gabriel Rossetti (1828–82), they soon expanded to include other like-minded painters, sculptors and writers. The Brotherhood was unusual in many ways. The very notion of a Brotherhood, something that valued the collective over the individual, went against normal practice at this time. So too was the accent on realism rather than learning how to paint from studying the great Italian Renaissance masters – such as Raphael. To uphold artists working before the late fifteenth century, before the time of Raphael

– to be pre-Raphaelite – was to deliberately question, if not directly insult, the status of academic painting and the teaching of the Royal Academy of Arts, the premier teaching establishment in England, who considered Raphael, Leonardo and Michelangelo as the artists to learn from.

It was not only their detailed depiction of nature that set them apart from their contemporaries but also their choice of subject matter. This concentrated on both contemporary and medieval stories, interspersed with religious subjects. Ford Madox Brown (1821–93), an artist who later became an active supporter of Morris and the Arts and Crafts Movement, exemplifies their concerns. Although he refused the invitation to join the short-lived Brotherhood (it was all but over by 1853) he, and others, continued to support Pre-Raphaelite ideals in art throughout his life. His painting *The Last of England*, completed in 1855, is a touching depiction of one of the social problems of the day – unemployment. It shows the emigration of a young family, believed to have been inspired by the emigration of one of the

Ford Madox Brown, *Chaucer at the Court of Edward III* (1851). Brown's imaginative reconstruction of medieval England often required careful research to get the details of costumes and furniture correct and unwittingly fed the appetite for goods from Morris & Co. (Public domain)

town and country as the balance of political power shifted from the latter to the former. If the followers of Millais looked at the social problems of living in the fast-growing cities of industrial England, the followers of Rossetti sought escape and refuge in the past whilst seeing it as a critique of contemporary society. It was from the romance of this medieval world, depicted with an exactitude that comes from artistic realism and historical research, and the writings of Ruskin, that so much of the Arts and Crafts Movement drew its inspiration.

## The Gothic Revival

The medievalizing of the Pre-Raphaelites was but part and parcel of an increasing nineteenth-century fascination with the medieval world and its imagined values that can also be seen in nineteenth-century architecture. This was the Gothic Revival and its fascination with the medieval was more than artistic. At its core lay some of the great religious and political debates of the day.

In the 1830s a theological movement arose within the Church of England, and centred on Oxford, that sought to return the increasingly liberal-minded Church of England to its earlier Catholic roots. The early nineteenth-century Church was dominated by the Anglican ritual, especially the importance of the sermon. Services, and therefore church interiors, were focused on the pulpit and not the altar. The prevailing style of architecture, Classicism, maintained a calm, chaste interior divided up by pews, many only available to those who paid and who often ensured their pews had the best position, not only to see the vicar but to be seen by the rest of the congregation. The churches were essentially designed on the auditory principle as large preaching boxes and so to this Oxford Movement were in need of reform. Also known as the Tractarians, due to the publication of tracts, or writings, about the issues of the day by famous figures such as Edward Pusey (1800–82), John Henry Newman (1801–90) and John Keble (1792–1866), this Oxford Movement

original Brotherhood, the sculptor Thomas Woolner (1825–92), to Australia. At around the same time he was also painting a medieval subject, *Chaucer at the Court of Edward III*. Despite the difference in subject matter, both are painted in great detail displaying the 'truth to nature' in vivid medieval colours that Ruskin argued for, and the Pre-Raphaelites strove to achieve. However, painting medieval subjects presented more problems than contemporary scenes. Here items such as costumes and furniture had to be researched and sourced and, in some cases, made from scratch, if the painting was to be realistic in its content as well as its style.

Increasingly these two wings of the Brotherhood – the modern and the medieval – went their separate ways, the realists of modern life following Millais, those of medieval romance lining up behind Rossetti. But the split between contemporary and medieval subjects went further and illuminates a rift between became a powerful vehicle for such reform and led to many individuals undergoing a crisis of faith, eventually renouncing the Anglian Church and converting to Catholicism.

Just as the Pre-Raphaelites sought to revitalize contemporary art by going back to an earlier medieval state, so many churchmen and theologians sought to renew the Church of England by going back to earlier religious practices. The increasing calls for Irish emancipation, effectively affording greater recognition to Roman Catholicism, also fed the appetite for reform and led to it also being labelled Anglo-Catholicism. The Tractarian reforms ushered in more elaborate services with attention directed back to the high altar and away from the pulpit. It necessitated greater attention to church design, decoration, and ritual centred on the altar. Necessarily this return to earlier forms of church service required the re-introduction of correct forms of dress, decoration, hymns, and most importantly architecture.

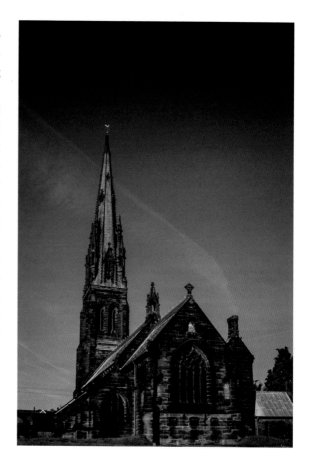

St Giles, Cheadle, Staffs. – the most convincing church of the Gothic Revival, hidden in a Staffordshire mining town. (Attribution-ShareAlike 2.0 Generic [CC BY-SA 2.0] © Brian Deegan)

## Pugin and the Gothic Revival

An important convert was a young architect, Augustus Welby Northmore Pugin (1812–52), raised in the Scottish Presbyterian faith but who converted to Catholicism in 1835. His father, Augustus Charles Pugin, was a Frenchman who fled the country during the Revolution. Trained as a draughtsman, he specialized in illustrating books on medieval Gothic architecture, such as *Specimens of Gothic Architecture* (1821) and trained his son in the same skill. Given his difficult upbringing, perhaps it is unsurprising to read of his reaction to churchgoing with his mother as a young boy. His friend Benjamin Ferry (1810–80) recalled that he '. . . always expressed unmitigated disgust at the cold and sterile forms of the Scottish church; and the moment he broke free from the trammels imposed on him by his mother, he rushed into the arms of a church which, pompous by its ceremonies, was attractive to his imaginative mind.'[31]

After a failed business venture – a decorating firm specializing in imaginative Gothic and Elizabethan interiors was probably too artistically advanced for the early 1830s – the son developed his career as a draughtsman and architect and was employed by Sir Charles Barry (1795–1860) on his competition-winning design of 1835 for the new Palace of Westminster.

Following his conversion, Christian meant Gothic and Gothic meant Catholic for Pugin. This strong stance, seen most clearly in the books he wrote after 1835, placed him in prime position to work for like-minded patrons such as John Talbot (1791–1852), the sixteenth Earl of Shrewsbury, and a leading Catholic aristocrat. The Earl first employed him on alterations and extensions to his country seat at Alton Towers in the Gothic Revival style from 1837, and then in 1847,

Painted stencil work to St Giles – when George Gilbert Scott saw it, the Earl of Shrewsbury said it 'absolutely made the water run down both sides of his mouth'. (Attribution-ShareAlike 2.0 Generic [CC BY-SA 2.0] © Michael Garlick)

The chancel roof as if 'powdered with gilt stars'. (Attribution-ShareAlike 2.0 Generic [CC BY-SA 2.0] © Michael Garlick)

commissioned him to design perhaps the finest church of the Gothic Revival, St Giles (1841–46), in nearby Cheadle, Staffordshire – a town peopled predominantly by miners and weavers. As his recent biographer, Rosemary Hill, has written, 'In its elaboration, its Englishness and its predominant symbolism . . . it was the epitome of Puginism.'[32] If the exterior, with its soaring spire and archaeologically accurate rendition of Pugin's favoured period of Gothic, is impressive for its date, its interior is a show-stopper. Pugin had spent some years working as a theatrical designer and for all its accuracy in recreating what he imagined the interior of a medieval church might have looked like – every surface covered in carving, gilding, stencils,

The Grange, Ramsgate – Pugin's own house, carefully and compactly planned, it became a model for later domestic architecture. (© Landmark Trust)

Pugin's rich Gothic Revival decoration of The Grange merges almost seamlessly with that of his adjacent church of St Augustine's, which he also designed. (© Landmark Trust)

If the work he did for Barry on the Houses of Parliament is his most iconic, and St Giles his most complete, his own house in Ramsgate, together with its private chapel, is also full of interest of a more personal nature as he devoted more thought to domestic architecture later in his career. Adjacent to St Augustine's (1845–52) – a church he paid for himself – construction of the house, called The Grange, began in 1843 and was completed in 1844, but the interior not until 1850, only two years before he died. However, Pugin's powerful championing of Gothic architecture was not confined to buildings.

In 1836 he wrote a book entitled *Contrasts; Or, A Parallel Between the Noble Edifices of the Fourteenth and Fifteenth Centuries and Similar Buildings of the Present Day. Shewing the Present Decay of Taste.* Although this long title accurately describes its method, it barely hinted at its intention. This was not merely architectural – to compare and contrast 'good' medieval architecture with the 'bad' Classical architecture of the time – but a determined attempt to persuade industrial Britain to return to the Catholic faith and the social structure of the Christian Middle Ages.

Further writings by Pugin, as great a polemicist as he was a designer, included ideas which informed the architects of the Arts and Crafts Movement in search of a simple, stripped-back style such his two 'great laws of design', namely that, 'There should be no features about a building which are not necessary for convenience, construction or propriety' and 'All ornament should consist of enrichment of the essential construction of the building.'[33] Whilst these theoretical ideas may seem hard to square with Pugin's elaborate practice, they embodied his ideas about truth in religion as in architecture. When the Arts and Crafts Movement sought examples of artistic integrity to support their own practice, they found it in abundance in the example of Pugin. Where Ruskin bequeathed the idea of 'truth to nature', it was Pugin who contributed the idea of 'honesty in construction' to them.

The relationship between the Gothic Revival and the architecture of the Arts and Crafts Movement

and decorative tiles – it is also a dramatic ensemble showing his debt not only to his father but to his earlier theatrical career in Covent Garden. Light filters not only through stained-glass windows (long since absent from the Anglican preaching boxes he hated) but polished metal screens, and then bounces back and forth between alabaster, marble and back to polished metal. That is not to say it is not also a deeply symbolic and religiously infused scheme of decoration designed with the utmost integrity. Pugin ties all his decoration back to Christian tracts and biblical allusions, which lie in wait for the devout to read. His own written account, *Lord Shrewsbury's New Church of St Giles, in Staffordshire* (1846), is almost as intoxicating as the experience of visiting the church, such as when he describes the chancel ceiling as 'powdered with gilt stars'.

Benjamin Woodward, Oxford University Union. The experience of working together under the direction of the Pre-Raphaelite artist D.G. Rossetti on the murals confirmed Morris' and Burne-Jones' decision to become artists.

The murals, now barely visible, enriched the upper wall surfaces of the Oxford University Union with Arthurian stories. Morris later decorated the roof in this light tone reminiscent of his 'Willow' wallpaper design.

was thus close and intimate. Both Webb and Morris had worked for the leading Gothic Revival architect George Edmund Street (1824–81). Meanwhile both Pugin and Ruskin (from different positions) promoted Gothic to a position of supposed unassailable moral superiority over all other styles. Hermann Muthesius also recognized the contribution that Gothic made. 'Clearly this movement was bound to merge with that of the Gothic Revival, for its range of ideas were similar,' he wrote and saw that the difference between the Gothic Revival and the Arts and Crafts Movement was that the Arts and Crafts architects were 'progressive rather than archaising'.[34]

## Gothic in Oxford: The university murals

This progressive Gothic can be seen in two buildings of the 1850s designed by Woodward and supported by Ruskin – the Oxford University Museum (already considered in the previous chapter) and the Oxford University Union – its debating society. In 1857 when the Oxford University Union extended its building by the addition of a debating chamber, it was suggested that its upper wall space be decorated with a series of murals depicting Arthurian themes. Ruskin commissioned Rossetti to undertake the work. The murals are spread over ten bays, each of which is pierced by a six-foiled Gothic window, and were painted between 1857 and 1859. Rossetti – working for expenses only – brought together six other artists, each of whom were given subjects from Malory's medieval poem *Morte d'Arthur* to depict. Painted directly onto the wall surface in vivid medieval colours (one admirer referred to them as being as beautiful as the margins of a medieval manuscript), it represents a coming together of Art and Architecture that was central to the Arts and Crafts Movement.

Ten years after the foundation of the Pre-Raphaelite Brotherhood, Rossetti had now distanced himself from it and this project effectively launched a second wave of Pre-Raphaelitism with himself as its leader – a baton that soon passed to Burne-Jones. It has been suggested that the seven artists who worked on the mural formed a sort of Arthurian 'round table' of artists, a second Brotherhood that in turn exercised an influence on later developments, such as the way the firm of Morris, Marshall, Faulkner and Company worked as a loose collaboration of artists, and even the establishment of groups such as the Centenary Guild, the Guild of Handicraft, and the Art Workers' Guild. For his part, Ruskin found the group painting the murals '. . . all the least bit crazy and it's very difficult to manage them.'[35] It was a bohemian image of the artist that Rossetti was eager to foster and may well have excited Edward Burne-Jones (1833–98) and William Morris to join him in painting the murals. Rossetti was equally excited and wrote to his friend William Bell:

> Two young men, projectors of the Oxford and Cambridge Magazine, have recently come up to town from Oxford, and are now very intimate friends of mine. Their names are Morris and Jones. They have turned artists instead of taking up any other career to which the university generally leads, and both are men of real genius.[36]

## William Morris

In the summer of 1854 Morris, whilst still a student, went to Belgium to study medieval art. In July 1855 he returned to Europe with Burne-Jones and William Fulford to travel across northern France, visiting nine cathedrals and twenty-four medieval churches. It was effectively a conversion not to Catholicism, but to art. As a result of the trip he and Burne-Jones committed themselves to a life of art. Both had studied

G.E. Street, the Church of St Philip and St James (1860–66), Oxford, shows the sort of work being designed by Street when Morris began his architectural training with him.

at Exeter College in Oxford, recently enlarged by the addition of a Gothic Revival chapel by George Gilbert Scott. Burne-Jones, and fellow student Fulford, were both from Birmingham and were part of the artistic group at Oxford at Pembroke College known as the 'Birmingham Set', which established the short-lived *Oxford and Cambridge Magazine* that so impressed Rossetti. As a result of their trip Morris decided to train as an architect; Burne-Jones as a painter. By the time of the murals Morris had begun his training in the Oxford office of George Edmund Street, writing to his mother that he thought the three-year regime would do him good, whilst Burne-Jones had gone to London where he was being taught by Rossetti.

Whilst Burne-Jones continued his training as a painter, Morris abandoned architecture after about eight months. Street had set him to work copying a drawing of a medieval doorway from Canterbury Cathedral and after eight months it seems his patience was worn out. Webb, Street's assistant, who looked after Morris during his training, suggested that Morris didn't take to architecture because, 'He found he could not get into close contact with it; it had to be done second hand.'[37]

Following his friend's example, Morris then turned to painting but found himself unsuited to this also, being unable to master figure-drawing. The writing on the back of his only easel painting, depicting his future wife Jane Burden as Queen Guinevere, put it well. 'I cannot paint you, but I love you', he wrote.

Morris came from a financially comfortable family background and attended public school at Marlborough College in addition to receiving private tuition. His father was a wealthy stock-broker who had done well out of investing in copper mines in Devon to the extent that Morris had an annual income of £700 to cushion him. It was whilst working on the murals that Rossetti and Burne-Jones spotted Morris's future wife, Jane Burden (1839–1914), in the theatre in Oxford one evening and encouraged her to sit for them as a model. When they married in Oxford in 1859, their house in rural Kent was designed by the former chief clerk in Street's office, Philip Webb.

If there was one thing Morris took from Street's office it was the beginnings of this important lifelong friendship with Webb that was central to the Arts and Crafts Movement. The two were in many ways polar opposites. Webb quiet, methodical, publicity shy, and doing most of the work in his office himself, helped by only one loyal assistant, George Jack (1855–1931). Morris was loud, rumbustious, impatient, proselytizing, and created circles of friends around him.

## Morris, Marshall, Faulkner & Co.

In preparation for moving into the Red House, their new marital home, in 1859 Webb and Burne-Jones designed and decorated a wardrobe, *The Prioress's Tale*, as a wedding present for the Morrises. The

*The Prioress's Tale* wardrobe by Burne-Jones and Webb. (© Ashmolean Museum, University of Oxford)

*Prioress's Tale* was a reference to one of Chaucer's *Canterbury Tales* – altogether not one of the happier tales. It was one of many substantial pieces of furniture the newlyweds eventually filled the house with, some coming from Burne-Jones and Morris's flat in Red Lion Square, others having to be specially made. The difficulty in finding such items (the problem shared with the Pre-Raphaelite artists in painting their medieval subjects) may well have been the spur to the foundation of Morris, Marshall, Faulkner and Co. – 'Fine Art Workmen in Painting, Carving, Furniture and the Metals' – in 1861. Their description of themselves is interesting in its determination to unite 'Fine Art' and 'Workmen' – in essence a forerunner of 'Arts and Crafts'. Apart from Morris the other founder members of the firm were the Pre-Raphaelite artists Brown and Rossetti, Webb, and then Morris's Oxford pals from the 'Birmingham Set' (also known as 'The Brotherhood') – Burne-Jones, Charles Faulkner (1833–92) and Peter Paul Marshall (1830–1900). Each of these

G.F. Bodley, All Saints, Selsley (1862). Bodley encouraged Morris and his associates to start their decorating company with the promise of work on such new churches.

seven founder members initially held nominal shares in the company of one pound, whilst Morris's mother – who had disapproved of him abandoning a religious or more conventional career after he graduated – contributed a loan of £100. Faulkner and Marshall are the less well-known names amongst the group. Faulkner, at Oxford with Morris and Burne-Jones, later became a respectable academic but in these early years was very much part of the slightly bohemian set. He painted one of the Union murals, helped decorate the Red House, designed for the firm and became its financial manager. In 1864 he resigned in favour of an academic career as he feared that the firm was not a commercially viable business. Marshall, a civil engineer, amateur painter and the outsider of the group, although a founder shareholder, seems to have contributed little despite designing some furniture and stained glass for the firm in its early years. However, according to Rossetti's brother, William, he may be the person who came up with the idea of the firm. Other sources suggest it was Brown, encouraged by promises of work from their friend the architect George Frederick Bodley (1827–1907).

One of the stained-glass windows by Morris, Marshall, Faulkner & Co. Note the clear and pale glass painted with delicate medieval patterns to allow more light through.

Keble College, Oxford, designed by William Butterfield – a tour de force of the bricklayer's art and a monument of the Anglo-Catholic Movement. The careful counterpoint of bands of stone with a variety of coloured brick created decoration that was part of the construction. In this way construction and decoration were impossible to separate and gave a new form of integrity to Victorian architecture. Art was not something applied later.

Once established, and within a year of being founded, the firm attracted favourable attention at the 1862 exhibition, the successor to the Great Exhibition of 1851. A variety of work was displayed including the *St George* cabinet, a piece of stout medieval-style furniture designed by Webb and painted by Morris similar in style to *The Prioress's Tale* and tapping into the fashionable vogue for 'art furniture' of the day. Webb was in many ways the firm's secret weapon in its early days by securing them contracts to decorate and furnish private houses such as Rounton Grange (1870–76) that he designed for wealthy clients like Sir Isaac Lowthian Bell (1816–1904). Church commissions came from

the network of Gothic Revival architects Webb knew through his master, Street, such as Bodley and Butterfield, so the firm covered the ecclesiastical market as well as the domestic. Other, more high-profile commissions came late in the 1860s with the Green Dining Room at the South Kensington Museum (it was only named the Victoria and Albert Museum in 1899) in 1866, and the redecoration of the Armoury and the Tapestry Room at St James's Palace (1866–67).

However, as Bodley had suggested, much of the firm's early success was not due to the secular domestic market but to the Church. The success of the Gothic Revival in architecture created a large market for stained glass and church decoration generally and Bodley turned out to be as good as his word, offering the firm a notable early commission for stained glass at Selsley, Gloucestershire in 1861–62. Here, the overall design of the scheme was prepared by Webb and then individual windows were designed by Burne-Jones, Rossetti, Brown and Morris himself. In contrast to the contemporary practice of filling the window space with coloured glass, here, especially to the triptychs to the south aisle, smaller coloured panels were set in fields of clear glass to admit as much light to the interior as possible. Burne-Jones and Brown generally drew the figures, Webb the birds and other animals, Morris the patterns that formed the background. Pattern design increasingly became Morris's forte as an artist – whether it was for wallpaper, textile, the borders of tapestries, or printed books.

This generation of Gothic Revival architects, although the inheritors of Pugin's work, were taking a different, less archaeologically accurate and more adventurous approach to the use of Gothic, seen most clearly in Butterfield's polychromatic chapel for Keble College, Oxford (1876). Contemporary with Selsley was St Michael and All Angels, Brighton (1860–61) also by Bodley and soon after, Street's St Martin-on-the-Hill in Scarborough of 1863. In the first ten years of the firm's existence around seventy-five per cent of their work was stained glass. However, as the firm developed (and Morris took control after 1875) it undertook more domestic commissions as the ecclesiastical market became depressed or, more likely, saturated.

## 'The House Beautiful'

One of the many spectacular interiors furnished by the firm was Wightwick Manor, Worcestershire in 1887. More Pre-Raphaelite and Aesthetic Movement than Arts and Crafts, its heavy Old English

style timber-framed architecture was designed by the Liverpool-based architect Edward Ould (1852–1909), its two-storey porch based on that of nearby Elizabethan Little Moreton Hall in Ould's native Cheshire. It is a good example of historicism in its adaptation of the local vernacular to create a modern home. Built adjacent to a modest seventeenth-century manor house (which was retained as servants' quarters) this revivalist exterior belies a jewel-like interior reflecting the advanced artistic tastes of the day and incorporates many of the firm's products. Designed for the wealthy Wolverhampton paint-manufacturer, Theodore Mander (1853–1900) and his appropriately named wife Flora Paint (1857/8–1905), the Manders were at the cutting edge of fashion when they were planning their new home, which, by employing great craftsmanship, cost an enormous £9,492.

On 10 May 1884, Theodore had attended a lecture in Wolverhampton on 'The House Beautiful' given by Oscar Wilde, one of the leaders of the Aesthetic Movement. Amongst three 'Rules for Art', reflecting Ruskinian ideas on art and craftsmanship, Wilde quoted approvingly Morris's dictum to have '. . . nothing in your houses that you do not know to be useful, or believe to be beautiful.' Theodore's notebook from the evening still exists. He wrote the saying down and took the message to heart in the choices he and

Wightwick Manor, Worcestershire. More revivalist than Arts and Crafts, nonetheless its owners valued the movement's progressive decorative forms, and possibly its political associations with more Liberal views.

his wife made over the decoration of the house, and in its later extension of 1897 that doubled the size of the original house. Hand-painted, richly coloured and glazed tiles by William De Morgan (1839–1917), a friend and associate of Morris who sold his ceramics through the company, are used to enrich the fireplaces in the drawing and morning rooms. A quote from Ruskin's *Modern Painters* is even carved into the wood panelling. Stained glass was supplied not by Morris but by Charles Kempe (one of Morris & Co.'s competitors and who, like them, had worked closely with Bodley), and the developing taste for antiques (often bought from farmhouse sales as industry drove rural depopulation) provided more furniture all offset with the fashionable craze for oriental blue and white china, and Eastern rugs. Wightwick is not a pure Arts and Crafts Movement house by any means but it is nonetheless an able demonstration of the type of clients drawn to Morris & Co., and how their products were used in a typical 'House Beautiful' of the wealthy middle-class business elite in the late nineteenth century.

The expense of Morris & Co. furnishings cannot be denied. For all his socialism these were not products for the working, or even artisan, class but the company did try to address a broad range of potential buyers. One of their best-known pieces of furniture, the lightweight so-called Sussex chair – of which several different versions were made – was probably designed for the firm by Brown in the mid-1860s. Turned on a lathe, it was priced in the company's catalogue at 9s and 9d, which compared favourably with other Arts and Crafts chairs. Certainly the company's manager, Warrington Taylor (1837–70) (who took over after Charles Faulkner resigned in 1864), is said to have liked it both for its 'poetry of simplicity' and modest price, believing that, 'It is hellish wickedness to spend more than 15/- on a chair, when the poor are starving in the streets.'[38]

The inglenook fireplace in the great parlour at Wightwick Manor. Despite the grandeur of many Arts and Crafts houses, the cosy inglenook became an essential feature of houses great and small – note the popular briar rose decoration above the fireplace. Talk of 'inglenookery' became a way of gently teasing the simple-life pretensions of the wealthy.

Elegant, lightweight, and affordable. The Sussex chair of 1865 is one of Morris & Co.'s most recognizable products. Based on a traditional pattern, its ebonized birch frame and exposed rush seating display the principles of honesty in materials and construction they promoted. (CC0 1.0 Universal, Public Domain Dedication)

The Red House, Bexleyheath, Kent – the garden front. When completed, such barefaced redness would have been shocking. Note the variety of window designs and complexity of different roof outlines – what happens on the inside is hinted at on the outside.

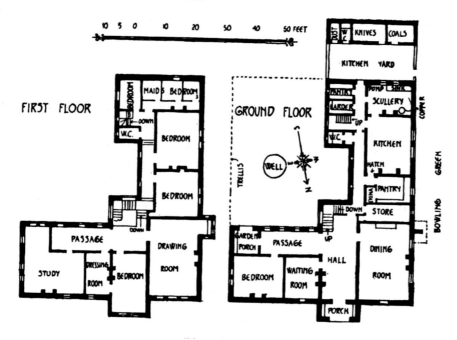

The Red House, Bexleyheath, must be considered the first building of the Arts and Crafts Movement. Writing many years after he left it, Morris told his friend Andreas Scheu, 'I got a friend to build me a house very medieval in spirit in which I lived for five years, and set to decorating it; we found, I and my friend the architect especially, that all the minor arts were in a state of complete degradation.'[39] Built between 1859 and 1860, at a cost of £4,000, it belongs to the origins of the movement and was the first house of the newly-wed William Morris and Jane Burden. It was also the first building designed by 'my friend', the architect Philip Webb after leaving the office of Street. Conceived of by Morris as a Tennysonian 'Palace of Art', its significance lies not only in the nature of its design but the character of its interior, its relationship to its garden setting and the world of medieval romance its owner created there.

Discussions about the house probably began on Morris's third trip to northern France in August 1858, accompanied this time by Webb. Webb sketched initial ideas on the back of a map they were using as they rowed along the Seine, and then developed the design over the next few months. Given Morris's fame and indefatigable industry (and perhaps interference) there has been much speculation about who actually designed the Red House – Webb, or Morris, or

both. Certainly Morris was not a back-seat client – that was simply not in his nature – and the design and oversight of its construction mattered greatly to him as the realization of his medieval ideals. To ensure he got what he wanted he rented a house nearby to live in during its construction, which also served as site hut and drawing office for Webb. However, all the drawings for the house, down to its finer details, are by Webb, the experienced architect. This personal involvement in every project, and eye for detail, was to be a feature of his work for the rest of his life, but more in the manner of the master mason on site than a professional architect working in a remote office.

Whatever the extent of the co-operation between Webb and Morris on the design of the building, there is no doubt that the furnishing and interior decoration was a group endeavour in the spirit of a medieval guild, or brotherhood, involving not only Webb and Morris, but Jane, Rossetti, Burne-Jones, and many of those who worked as designers for Morris, Marshall, Faulkner & Co. As his biographer, J.W. Mackail, wrote in 1899, 'Not a chair, or table, or bed; not a cloth or paper hanging from the walls; nor tiles to line fireplaces or passages; nor a curtain or a candlestick; nor a jug to hold wine or glass to drink it out of, but had to be reinvented.'[40]

Why Red? It would seem obvious. Everywhere you look is the rich red brick and tile – and without any relief or contrast supplied by a different shade of red, let alone a different colour as was then becoming fashionable in the polychromatic work of Street and Butterfield. Yet ironically Webb's choice of red brick is one of the few criticisms that can be made of the house. Webb's subsequent practice as an architect was to use local materials, to make the building reflect the very land it was built on, and out of which it was constructed. In a Ruskinian sense he went to nature so that, for example, the colour of the bricks related to that of the local clay and therefore reflected the regional character of the local architecture. However, had that been the case here the house would have been called something like the Light Brown House, or the Buff House, as that is the colour of brick that results from using the local Kentish clay. But that would hardly have been catchy. The redness and unrelieved nature of the brick is partly a radical statement. No amount of ornament or external decorative details detract from its construction. It is honest in its use of brick; indeed, it glories in it with no attempt to disguise its everyday character by covering it with stucco or any other material as was common on villas for the middle and upper classes of the day. Webb glories in it and uses it as a device to link interior and exterior.

Once seen on the outside it carries through to the inside, breaking out overhead in the relieving arches, door heads, and symbolically for all the fireplaces – it's as if the material formed by fire becomes fireplaces to make you appreciate how brick is made. Additionally, each fireplace displays a different method of bricklaying, so revelling in the craft skill of the bricklayer's art. The redness of the house also flows onto the heavy terracotta tiles of the floor, bringing the external garden paths into the internal circulation spaces. So there is a consistent truth to materials, a truth to nature, and an honesty in construction found from inside to outside here.

If its basic unit of construction – the standard-size brick – is simple, other aspects of the building are not and display Webb's early understanding of construction to suggest age and connect with a variety of traditional building techniques. The roofs, for example, are a complex, intersecting series of shapes and construction types dictated partly by the rooms and spaces they protect, partly to create a romantic profile, and partly to suggest shelter. This varied zig-zag outline is then heightened by the use of the lead finials, pennants, and weather-vanes that are scattered across the roofscape. The windows are no less varied, being a mixture of casements, dormers, sash windows, circular, and open and

One of the brick fireplaces in the Red House. Medieval in spirit and demonstrating the skill of the bricklayer, it displays how Webb also united the outside of the house with the inside through his handling of the material.

fixed glazing, all of a size and shape to light the spaces as required. The external impression must have seemed bizarre, or unfinished, in its day. House design was not seen as an area for architectural experimentation to this extent.

One of the few other criticisms levelled against the Red House is the location of the fireplaces against outside walls, which

caused problems for the chimney stacks' ability to draw smoke out of the building. Although the image of the medieval open-hall house with a fire burning in the middle of the floor and the smoke gradually escaping through the thatched roof may have beguiled the romantically minded Arts and Crafts Movement, a room full of smoke was perhaps going too far. Webb later heightened the stacks

Details of the brickwork to the oriel window – craftsmanship exposed rather than covered with stucco to imitate stone.

Baldersby St James, Yorkshire. William Butterfield designed not only the church in the background (and its vicarage) but also a variety of houses and the village school in a simple, unaffected manner that the Arts and Crafts Movement admired.

Saints', Maidenhead (1854–57) and Baldersby St James (1855–57). Webb would have known the type well as they were the essential accompaniment to Street's churches, which he had worked on as his chief assistant. Their simplicity concealed a hierarchy of decoration and careful construction. The church was the most important building, and within the church the east end, so that received the most elaborate and expensive decoration. Then came the vicarage and ancillary buildings – perhaps a school or village hall – and finally the estate houses. The less status, the less decoration. Lower down the hierarchy then could be found buildings that were well-designed for their function, nicely proportioned to relate to their church, and simple and unostentatious in their decoration. It is this tradition that the Red House relates to. It is an irony that as both Burne-Jones and Morris had been intending to take holy orders before coming under the influence of art, that they would have possibly ended up living in such a vicarage. But then at Bexleyheath we begin to see art raised to the level of religion – the world of medieval beauty being an escape from the uglier aspects of industrial Britain.

and rarely made the same mistake again.

In many ways the Red House was a private showroom of the most advanced artistic ideas of the day, a sort of testing ground for the Arts and Crafts Movement for its sturdy copies of medieval painted furniture. In addition to their wedding presents and other purpose-designed pieces, such as the settle in the hallway, new items from Morris, Marshall, Faulkner & Co. followed. The interior gradually filled with medieval-inspired furniture, murals, hangings, light-fittings, and stained glass. It became,

as Rossetti (a frequent visitor to the house) later recalled, 'more a poem than a house'.[41]

However radical it was in its simplicity, it was not unique but rather the development of a new tradition. This was the genre of the mid-Victorian vicarage – the type of building begun by Pugin in his family house St Marie's Grange, Alderbury (1835–37), then developed at the Grange, Ramsgate (1844), and finally in rectories such as at Rampisham, Dorset (1847). It was taken up by the likes of Street, Bodley and Butterfield in buildings such as those at All

In shunning Classical architecture, the Red House is designed on a Gothic-inspired, additive picturesque principle of planning which sees discrete elements of the building – porch, service wing, stair

Webb once said that, 'To draw animals you must sympathize with them; you must know what it feels like to be an animal.' One of his fresh contemporary window designs here contrasts with the more medieval-inspired work of Morris, Rossetti, and others.

Morris's design for his 'Trellis' wallpaper of 1862 was partly inspired by the gardens at the Red House and features a briar rose design favoured by his friend Edward Burne-Jones. (Wikimedia Commons. Public domain)

turret, oriel window, studio and so on – expressed externally and separately to suggest the internal functions. This ability to 'read' the building in functional terms is reinforced by the size, shape, and positioning of windows no less than the interplay of roof forms. Many years later this aspect of the Red House – that it may be seen as having been designed from the inside out – was seen as an early instance of functionalism – the Modernist approach to architecture famously expressed as 'form follows function' by the American architect Louis Sullivan in 1896, thirty-six years after the Red House was completed. Although there is no denying the fact of this interpretation, it has perhaps tended to ignore much of the rich imaginative decorative scheme in

favour of post-rationalizing the design and so claiming Webb as an early Modernist. This, it might be thought, is dangerously ahistorical and denies the significance of the building in its day.

Now largely devoid of much of that richness, luckily here and there important elements of decoration survive. Most notable is the stained glass designed by Webb and Burne-Jones, and made by Morris. Here, once sacred imagery becomes secular through Webb's delightful drawings of animals. Similarly, the two simple vernacular patterns painted to the ceilings – executed free-hand following a pattern picked out in the wet plaster as found above the main staircase – are examples of both

honesty and the timeless vernacular tradition. In contrast are the painted murals commissioned from Burne-Jones. In the drawing room were meant to be seven wall paintings based on the medieval romance of Sir Degrevant. Elsewhere Burne-Jones was also supposed to have painted scenes from the Trojan Wars on the walls of the staircase hall. It is ironic that for a man now so associated with wallpaper, so little was used in the Red House. Although the garden of the Red House, and its carefully maintained orchard, inspired his first wallpaper design, Trellis, of 1862, Morris didn't favour wallpaper for his own house. It was perhaps too modern an invention and he strove instead to create a medieval ambiance by the use of

The front elevation, with its pointed Gothic entrance, nods to Pugin's earlier work but could easily pass for a new Gothic Revival vicarage by Butterfield, Bodley or Street.

The carved newel posts to the main staircase show the clear debt of the Arts and Crafts Movement to the Gothic Revival. The bare walls were to have been enriched with a large mural painting.

hangings or murals, as would have been found in medieval buildings.

Despite seeking to avoid overt expressions of famous styles from the past there is no escaping elements of Gothic in the Red House, and Morris himself described it as 'in the style of the thirteenth century'. Hence the front door is set behind a porch dominated by a pointed arch, the elongated wooden newel posts to the main staircase are simply carved Gothic pinnacles with crenellations, and the style of some of the stained glass is no different from that the firm used in Gothic Revival churches. The furniture also contributed to the medieval spirit and even included a settle in the drawing room originally painted with scenes by Rossetti, including his famous painting *Dantis Amor*, as a further wedding present. It was later extended by Webb to form a mini minstrels' gallery but with the added bonus of giving access to the roof space.

Externally the L-shaped plan of the house – with the well-lit servants' range to the south – allows the easy creation of a further symbol of shelter as the two wings of the building protect a carefully designed well which forms a focal point to this more private side of the house. To one end is the kitchen; to the other the Pilgrim's Rest porch, lined with hand-painted tiles by Morris containing his family motto '*Si je puis*' ('If I can') with a built-in bench seat.

Originally painted dragon red to aid the medieval richness of the interior, this settle – the upper cupboards originally enclosed by doors with medieval paintings by Rossetti – also provides a mini minstrels' gallery that gives access to the loft hatch behind. Note the section of surviving mural painting to the right.

The name of the porch connects with the history of the site – the Pilgrim's Way to Canterbury lies not far from the Red House – a perfect location symbolically for Morris. Symbolism enters again when looking at the anthropomorphic profile of the oriel window – where Jane Morris could sit with her embroidery recalling the poem of Tennyson's *Mariana in the Moated Grange* – a favourite topic of the Pre-Raphaelites.

There are many accounts of how the Morrises lived at the Red House – often an open, rumbustious household with Morris as both Lord of the Manor and Court Jester. From here he could conduct business in London, taking a pony and trap from the carriage house designed by Webb

to the nearby railway station. His great friends Edward and Georgina Burne-Jones were regular visitors. Georgina recalled that, 'It was the most beautiful sight in the world to see Morris coming up from the cellar before dinner, beaming with joy, and his hands full of bottles of wine and others tucked under his arms'.[42] The house was intended to have an extension in the form of a third wing. This would have further enclosed the well and provided a home for the Burne-Joneses, and a studio for Edward, thus creating a form of communal artistic living as advanced by the bohemian lifestyle pursued by the Pre-Raphaelites, '. . . all the least bit crazy', as Ruskin said.

In 1864 two disasters struck – one financial, another personal. The

firm was struggling to survive and Morris was considering moving the business. This put a considerable strain on Morris and on his marriage to Jane. This was already troubled by a relationship between her and Rossetti. Secondly, the Burne-Jones's son caught scarlet fever, which he passed onto his then pregnant mother. The result was the early death of their prematurely born new child after only three weeks. The sadness was immense, the Burne-Joneses decided not to move out to Upton, the Morrises also became unwell, and everything seemed to be threatening Morris's happy communal life at the Red House. In 1865 the Morrises sold up and a heartbroken William never returned. The new brotherhood he had sought to create in his palace of art, his Camelot, was broken. The house then passed through the hands of others to appreciate its uniqueness and importance, including Charles Holmes (1868–1936), the proprietor of *The Studio*, and finally Ted Hollamby (1921–99), an Arts and Crafts enthusiast, fellow socialist, and architect for public bodies such as the Miners' Welfare Commission and London County Council, who left it to the National Trust. Given its importance to the architecture of the Arts and Crafts Movement, it is almost a modern pilgrimage site in its own right.

# Chapter 3

# Forming a Movement

A S WE HAVE SEEN, MANY OF THE IDEAS that led to the creation of the Arts and Crafts Movement can be traced back to the growing nineteenth-century fascination with medieval life, whether through the paintings of the Pre-Raphaelites, or the buildings of the Gothic Revival, both championed and channelled through the powerful contemporary writings of Ruskin. This chapter considers how theory turned into practice and how key organizations and groupings led to the appearance of the Arts and Crafts Movement in the1880s. These were the Society for the Protection of Ancient Buildings, the Art Workers' Guild, the Arts and Crafts Exhibition Society, and the Memorialists. The first came into being in 1877, the last in 1891, and it is noticeable how the same set of individuals crop up again and again to form a network of Arts and Crafts intelligentsia in London. Alongside these new radical organizations sat the older professional associations of the Royal Academy of Arts, and the Royal Institute of British Architects. These two bodies very much represented the establishment of their day and were the bodies against which the Arts and Crafts Movement came to define itself between these dates.

Opposite: The wooden gate to the courtyard at Standen is held back in the afternoon sun. The colourful imperfection of the stone corbel that connects the gate pier with the roof beam was the sort of detail Webb delighted in. The gateway was devised as an architectural way to unite the old farmhouse on the site to the new house.

## The Society for the Protection of Ancient Buildings

In the thirty-three years between 1840 and 1873, a survey of church building and restoration carried out by Parliament found that around 7,000 medieval churches in England and Wales had been restored, rebuilt, or enlarged. This is an astonishing number and a clear indication of the scale of the problem the Society for the Protection of Ancient Buildings came into existence to address. Restoration was an increasing source of debate in the nineteenth century, especially given the increasing fascination with medieval life. SPAB, as it became known, was adamantly against the practice of restoration and in favour rather of protection, of leaving things alone more than intervening. The difference may seem slight but was vitally important. As Ruskin succinctly put it, 'better a crutch than a lost limb'.[43] In his writings he created the idea of the 'stewardship' of ancient buildings, arguing in 'The Lamp of Memory', one of the chapters of his *Seven Lamps of Architecture* (1849), that, 'We have no right whatever to touch them. They are not ours. They belong partly to all the generations of mankind who are to follow us.'[44] Ruskin argued strongly that it was age, more than condition, and perhaps even artistry, that was the reason to protect ancient buildings. 'Its glory', he wrote of an ancient building, 'is in its Age, and in that deep sense of voicefulness, of stern watching, of mysterious sympathy, nay, even of approval or condemnation, which we feel in walls that have long been washed by the passing waves of humanity.'[45]

The seminal case that led to the creation of SPAB in 1877 was George Gilbert Scott's proposed restoration of Tewkesbury Abbey. This provoked a letter of outrage by Morris being published in *The Athenaeum* on 10 March 1877. He wrote, 'Is it altogether too late to do something to save it – it and whatever else beautiful or historical is still left us of the sites of the ancient buildings. . . ?' Debate continued in lively fashion in the letters pages of *The Times* and Morris included in one of his the suggestion of creating '. . . an association for the purposes of watching over and protecting these relics'. Webb, similarly aroused, wrote to his friend the artist George Price Boyce (1826–97) on 15 March 1877 also suggesting that some sort of society should be formed to fight what was seen as the new vandalism, although he admitted he was '. . . not, however, anticipating any great success.'[46]

Despite Webb's scepticism, the Society for the Protection of Ancient Buildings was duly founded and was quickly nicknamed, appositely, 'Anti-Scrape' by Morris. This was an honest enough name for a society opposed to the scraping clean of old buildings by removing plasterwork and weathered stone in order to 'restore' the building back to a sharper, cleaner appearance that was thought to be more like its original condition. On its foundation it published a manifesto written by Morris, Webb and others but with strong echoes of Ruskin in every line. It repays careful reading but its central argument was Ruskin's from *The Lamp of Memory*, that restoration was 'a strange and most fatal idea, which by its very name implies that it is possible to strip from a building this, that, and the other part of its history – of its life that is – and then to stay the hand at some arbitrary point, and leave it still historical, living, and even as it once was.'

In place of restoration, SPAB urged that architects should '. . . put Protection in the place of Restoration, to stave off decay by daily care, to prop a perilous wall or mend a leaky roof by such means as are obviously meant for support or covering, and show no pretence of other art, and otherwise to resist all tampering with either the fabric or ornament of the building as it stands.'

Burford church, Gloucestershire. The restoration of the church by G.E. Street outraged Morris and was one of the cases that led to the creation of the SPAB.

The initial development of these ideas can be seen in Morris's growing exasperation over the restoration of medieval churches. As early as 1855 we find him writing to his friend Cromwell Price, '. . . we went to see Ely, which disappointed me somewhat, it is so horribly spoilt with very well meant restorations, as they facetiously term them.'[47] Twenty years later, travelling from his home in Kelmscott in September 1876, Morris came across restoration work being undertaken on the medieval church of St John the Baptist, Burford. The architect in charge was his old master, Street. Amongst the works being done was the cutting back of areas of decayed stonework, the very practice SPAB was to abhor, involving as it did the destruction of what Ruskin saw as the 'face of the past' with all its changes, decay, alterations and weathering that he found to be of such value. Although Morris remonstrated with the vicar he was effectively sent

Rather than demolish the old house at Forthampton Court, Webb added new extensions using the SPAB philosophy of 'keeping in keeping' to blend the new work with the old.

away with a flea in his ear by the incumbent and told to mind his own business as, against Ruskin's idea of stewardship, came the more usual argument that, 'The church, Sir, is mine; and if I choose to, I shall stand on my head in it.'[48]

As ever Webb and Morris worked as a team – Morris vociferous and combative, Webb quietly getting on with the job in hand. Webb came to play the leading architectural role in SPAB in developing conservative conservation techniques to retain as much original fabric of a building as possible. Using aspiring young architects such as Detmar Blow and Alfred Powell (1865–1960), he developed techniques that also as a consequence began to unpick how traditional buildings had been constructed in the first place. Yet there were limits to protection and sometimes he refused to work on churches that he felt had suffered enough intervention already. In relation to domestic buildings he sometimes adopted a more nuanced approach. Compared to churches, houses were more numerous and, practically, had to continue functioning and adapting to changing family life.

This difference can be clearly seen at Forthampton Court, Gloucestershire. Here the owner, John R. Yorke (1836–1912), intended to demolish and extend his property. Initially he approached the architect William Burges (1827–81) who had already designed the village almshouses for him. Then, possibly after seeing his friend Percy Wyndham's new house, Clouds, designed by Webb, he approached him. After inspecting the medieval building Webb refused to demolish or even make serious alterations to the house – save for a 'modern' few Georgian elements. The house had been the residence of the Abbots of Tewkesbury and was a palimpsest of historical layers developing over the centuries. Instead he repaired the existing fabric and added a new entrance front with additional bedrooms in a tower block, and a new laundry block signalled by prominent gables that became so characteristic of his work. When complete, the client was so pleased with the results that he became a member of SPAB, and Webb in response took the family on a shopping expedition to the showrooms of Morris & Co. to select the new furnishings – they were paying. Clearly John Yorke became a firm convert not only to the works of the Arts and Crafts Movement but also to conservation as in 1900 he halted further damaging restoration proposals at nearby Tewkesbury Abbey – the 'foundation' building that led to the creation of SPAB in the first place. Conservation work such as this – the extension of existing buildings – was to become a significant aspect of Webb and his growing number of admirers amongst the younger generation.

Within twenty years the society had attracted over 400 members. Meetings of its Committee were held regularly and afterwards, as Lethaby recalled, they would all retire to eat together at Gatti's, an Italian restaurant on the Strand in London. Lethaby also recalled how happy its members, the second generation of Arts and Crafts architects – including himself, Ernest Gimson and Alfred Powell – were when Morris was absent and they had their beloved Webb all to themselves. Lethaby (first taken to a SPAB meeting by his good friend Gimson) saw SPAB's importance as much greater than trying to protect ancient buildings from over-zealous architects, aristocrats and clergy-men. He wrote in his biography of Gimson, 'Dealing as it did with the common facts of traditional building in scores and hundreds of examples it became under the technical guidance of Webb, the architect, a real school of practical *building* – architecture with all the whims which we usually call design left out.'[49]

## The Art Workers' Guild and the rediscovery of the arts connected with building

The experience of working on old buildings developed an awareness of disappearing craft skills and led directly to the Arts and Crafts' most important organization – the Art Workers' Guild. Founded in 1884 the form of words used in the title – like Morris & Co.'s 'Fine Art Workmen' over twenty years earlier – is redolent of its idealism. It grew out of two architects' offices – J.D. Sedding's and Norman Shaw's – and two existing societies – The Fifteen and the St George's Art Society.

According to Walter Crane, The Fifteen started meeting in the winter of 1881. The name is confusing – and membership never reached fifteen – that being the name of a popular puzzle of the day. Other members included Henry Holiday (1839–1927), George Blackall Simonds (1843–1929), Hugh Stannus (1840–1908) and Walter Crane. Primarily a decorative arts society, it met monthly between May and October in members' London houses. Its leader was the decorative artist Lewis F. Day (1845–1910). Initially trained as a stained-glass artist, Day's work came to embrace tiles, furniture, wallpaper, carpets, textiles and the whole gamut of the decorative arts that were connected with building. He was also a writer and lecturer, and like his friend Walter Crane, a tireless promoter of the decorative arts.

Shortly after its formation in 1883, a group of architects and pupils from Shaw's office formed a similar discussion group, the St George's Art Society – so called because it met after work in the shadow of St George's Church, Bloomsbury, in the offices of Ernest Newton (1856–1922) in Hart Street. Arthur Mackmurdo suggested the name also had more than a nod of deference to Ruskin's earlier Guild of St George about it. Committee members included Ernest Newton, Mervyn Macartney (1853–1932), Reginald Barratt (1861–1917), Edwin Hardy, Gerald Horsley (1862–1917), Lethaby and E.J. May (1853–1941) (the only committee member who was not from Shaw's office) – all under thirty years old. After a while Shaw encouraged his acolytes to reconsider their society's purpose and to refocus their attention on 'the unity of all the arts'.

## Naming names

So similar were the two groups in their interests that in 1883 merger discussions took place. These were in part also informed by growing disquiet about the stance of the Royal Academy towards architecture and the crafts. That year its Summer Exhibition seemed to snub the so-called 'mother of the arts' and it was somewhat ignominiously relegated to two side walls of one gallery.

As with any merger the new name was an issue. The architect turned metal worker, W.A.S. Benson

The logo devised for the Art Workers' Guild by Walter Crane in 1902. Note the artist's witty incorporation of his initials with the outline of a crane.

(1854–1924), initially suggested that the new combined group be called the Guild of Art. This certainly had the benefit of invoking the guild idea which was so central to their aims, and the lofty status of art. Additional names were suggested such as the Guild of Associated Arts, Guild of Art Workers, the Art Workers, and the Society of Art Workers. Edward Prior refined them all to become the Art Workers' Guild – and the title was accepted at the meeting of 11 March 1884. Prior also wrote the guild's prospectus. The guild's first formal meeting was held in 1884 and, like a guild, it was presided over by a Master – initially George Blackall Simonds from The Fifteen, but subsequently Sedding (1886) and then Crane (1888). Its motto – following Morris and Shaw – was 'Art is Unity'.

This radical new organization was founded in 1884 and described itself as being created '. . . with the object of bringing into closer union the workers in various arts and crafts – architects, painters, designers of all kinds, sculptors and wood-carvers, metal-workers, goldsmiths, and many others – chiefly by evening meetings and discussions on different lines and methods in art.' Meetings were held every two weeks when papers were read followed by lively discussion. As many committee members of the guild were also on the committee of SPAB, the movement's network was broadening and strengthening and by 1890 guild membership had risen to 150 and included many of the finest artists and craftsmen of the day.

Being deliberately 'shy' of publicity (as unprofessional), the Art Workers' Guild held few exhibitions for its members to display their work but rather restricted itself to lectures, demonstrations, and outings. The main benefit to all its members was bringing the increasingly remote architect into closer contact with the craftsmen and the 'arts connected with building' so as to better understand the whole process of how a building was constructed. In essence, the guild was a forum for the exchange of ideas – but ideas that could be acted on and even change lives. This is seen by many of its members – such as Benson, Gimson, and the Barnsley brothers – becoming accomplished craftsmen happy to collaborate on buildings with friends such as Lethaby, Webb and Prior, to name but a few. With the network of architect-craftsmen established, and a deeper understanding of the processes by which a building was created, architecture was capable once again of becoming the more collaborative endeavour it was thought to have been before industrialization, in the era when craft guilds dominated and built the great medieval cathedrals of Europe.

## The guild ideal – early beginnings

The idea of guilds, brotherhoods, collective working and communal living was a strong current in the Arts and Crafts Movement and it came in many shapes and sizes. One type of forerunner was of course the Pre-Raphaelite Brotherhood, which embraced a similarly anonymous group identity. 'The Brotherhood' was also the name adopted by the group of undergraduates at Oxford, also known as The Birmingham Set, which published *The Oxford and Cambridge Magazine*. And Ruskin, an admirer of both 'brotherhoods', developed his own Guild of St George in 1878 out of his earlier St George's Company of 1871. This was an ambitious venture into which Ruskin, the self-styled 'Master' of the guild, donated the considerable sum of £7,000. With the money, the guild established a museum in Sheffield where the city's cutlery workers could develop their creativity. It also bought land nearby which was run on a co-operative basis as a market garden, supported the revival of the cottage industries in the Lake District, inspired the donation of eight cottages in Barmouth for craft workers, and much, much else.

## The example of Mackmurdo and Ashbee

Arthur Heygate Mackmurdo began studying architecture in 1869. In his early years he worked for the Gothic Revival architect James Brooks (1825–1901) but crucially also started to attend Ruskin's drawing classes in Oxford. A founder member of SPAB after accompanying Ruskin on a tour of Italy, he offered to teach for him in his Sheffield-based guild. This experience quickly led to him establishing his own, the Century Guild in 1882. Its purpose was 'to render all branches of art the sphere no longer of the tradesman but the artist', and together with his architectural partner, Herbert Horne (1864–1916), and Selwyn Image (1849–1930) it also published an influential

C.R. Ashbee drawn by William Strang in 1903. (Wikimedia Commons. Public domain)

Brooklyn, Mackmurdo's house for his brother in Enfield designed in 1883, plays fast and loose with the classical language of architecture and is an early example of a flat-roofed building. (Courtesy of Stuart Evans.)

A.S. Dixon's Guild of Handicraft building in Birmingham shows a clear debt to Philip Webb. (Courtesy of Andy Foster)

journal, *The Century Guild Hobby Horse*. Image also attended Ruskin's drawing classes and, like Morris and Burne-Jones, abandoned the Church for a career as an artist. Mackmurdo and the Century Guild produced a range of decorative goods such as furniture, wallpaper, light fittings, embroidery, stained glass and book plates until it was dissolved in 1888.

Ironically the year it was dissolved was also the year that Charles Robert Ashbee (1863–1942) established the Guild and School of Handicraft in Whitechapel in London's East End. At the time he was a resident in Toynbee Hall, one of the earliest university settlements in the country. These were established to help educate the adult working class by establishing halls, based on the residential halls of Oxford and Cambridge, where university graduates and other educated members of the middle class would live alongside locals as a social experiment to spread the benefits of their education. Initially it was successful but as national educational reforms began to kick in, and classes in the arts and crafts were established by local authorities, a private venture like Ashbee's school could no longer compete, and the profits from selling the work of the guild were insufficient to keep it going. With the establishment of London County Council's Central School of Arts

and Crafts an increasingly bitter Ashbee made the dramatic decision to move his workforce of 200 craftsmen and their families to Chipping Camden in rural Gloucestershire and re-establish the guild there in 1902.

Birmingham fared better than London in managing to sustain a guild. Under the guidance of the architect and silversmith A.S. Dixon (1856–1929) it established the Birmingham Guild of Handicraft, which had as its motto 'By hammer and hand'. Dixon both taught at the school and designed its impressive building in 1898 – looking like an enormous version of the Red House – and had close links with Edward Taylor (1838–1911), the headmaster of the progressive Birmingham School of Art. The more one looks at the Arts and Crafts Movement, the more one trips over guilds – big and small, professional and amateur – and it's clear that this medieval model for organizing work was highly attractive to them and grounded in Ruskin's original example. However, the Art Workers' Guild was different from all these guilds. Whilst they sought to teach, make and sell, the Art Workers' Guild was more of a national London-based organization to maintain, revive and spread knowledge of the crafts amongst its members for the benefit of society at large. Combining the same functions as its parent, the Northern Art Workers' Guild (1896–1911) nonetheless more readily embraced the idea of exhibitions. Created, yet again, by the tireless Walter Crane, it was led by the hugely talented Edgar Wood.

## Going public – The Arts and Crafts Exhibition Society

Despite considerable reticence on the part of many of its members, within two years of the foundation of the Art Workers' Guild, Walter Crane and Holman Hunt were discussing a national exhibition to popularize the work of the guild. Increasing dissatisfaction with the attitude of the Royal Academy of Arts was boiling over and many guildsmen wanted to mount exhibitions to give a voice to architecture and the decorative arts that were being ignored by the Royal Academy.

Walter Crane, in *An Artist's Remembrances*, recalled the year when there were a large number of rejections of guildsmen's work. He wrote, 'In the summer and autumn of 1886 things looked really more serious. Complaints were loud and deep from disappointed artists and their friends, and grew into something like a clamour.' However, the suggestion of mounting their own exhibition was not received well by some of its members who took the guild idea, and its inherent secrecy, very seriously. They had been badly embarrassed over the mosaics designed by one of the guildsmen for St Paul's Cathedral which, praised by some, were then officially censored by the guild, and many feared a repeat of this debacle.

Behind the scenes discussions were taking place with the Royal Academy to bring about the kind of reforms guild members wanted to encourage and recognize the so-called 'arts not fine'. It was a case of too little, too late. These discussions came to nothing and in 1887 a committee was formed, with Benson at its centre, which proposed to hold exhibitions of the crafts. Other committee members included Sedding, Heywood Sumner (1853–1940), Henry Longden, Emery Walker (1853–1931) and Lewis F.

Walter Crane's design for the Arts and Crafts Exhibition Society catalogue shows the artist and the craftsman shaking hands as a sign of unity. Their dress and tools make their different social status all too clear. (Author's collection)

Day. Originally this new society was to be called 'The Combined Arts', but the 'Arts and Crafts Exhibition Society' was the title eventually agreed on as suggested by the bookbinder T.J. Cobden Sanderson. Morris, although never wholly convinced of the wisdom of 'going public', spoke at its first exhibition and went on to give one of his most influential lectures, on Gothic architecture, for the new society. In a letter of 31 December 1887, he outlined his many misgivings, asking who was to 'find the money' and predicting that attendance would be low 'after the first week or two' since 'the public don't care one damn about the arts and crafts'.[50] He added that while Crane and Burne-Jones's works would be 'worth looking at', the rest 'would tend to be of an amateurish nature, I fear.' In conclusion, Morris wrote, 'I rather dread the said exhibition.'

The first exhibition was held at the recently opened New Gallery, Regent Street, London, in 1888 and its first president, and designer of the catalogue cover, was Walter Crane who remained its president until

Architecture was hard to exhibit. Here the architect Lionel F. Crane made use of a model to exhibit his 'small country house'. (*The Architectural Review*, July 1899)

1912. The New Gallery had recently taken over from the Grosvenor Gallery as the venue for radical new art in London. One of the radical departures for the exhibition was the determination that not only the designer of the objects on display, but the maker, the craftsman, the art-worker, should also be acknowledged. At its first exhibition a staggering 517 items were displayed. Ashbee took Bodley to the exhibition, who remarked, 'I seem to see the ghosts of all my former friends.'[51]

Initially the society's exhibitions were eagerly and enthusiastically visited and reviewed by supportive magazines such as *The Studio* and *The Architectural Review*, and it issued its own proselytizing publications including *Arts and Crafts Essays by Members of the Arts and Crafts Exhibition Society* (1893), which provides a useful summary of what had been achieved in its first five years. However, Morris's words proved to be prophetic as later exhibitions proved to be less successful. When Henry Wilson (1864–1934) took over as president in 1912 he briefly reinvigorated its flagging spirits by succeeding in holding an exhibition of the society's work at the Royal Academy. Finally, the bastion of the Academy was breached. Even greater recognition for the crafts followed with a triumphant exhibition in Paris, at the Louvre, which boasted 1,625 exhibits. Disrupted by the outbreak of the First World War, and with many of the exhibits subsequently kept

in store in France, it wasn't until 1916 that it found its voice again in an exhibition in London.

Through SPAB feeding into the Art Workers' Guild, and the work of the Arts and Crafts Exhibition Society in promoting the crafts, the obstruction of the Royal Academy had, it seems, been taken care of. Now only the Royal Institute of British Architects remained as a barrier to the recognition of the architect-craftsmen. Their opposition came to a head in what became known as the 'Profession or Art debate'.

## The Memorialists and 'The Profession or Art debate'

In its attempts to secure work and status for its members similar to the established professions of Medicine and the Law, the Institute of British Architects (as it was originally known at the time of its foundation in 1834) nursed a long-cherished ambition to legally control who could, and crucially, who could not call themselves architects. This title they wanted to be defined by law, based on an agreed system of education, which could be examined (the examiners were to be the institute and its senior members) and the successful individual architects' names placed on a publicly accessible register. To many members of the movement the very idea that art (which they considered architecture to be) could be examined was anathema. As there was no agreed definition on what an architect's duties were, the institute had a large number of members who were more readily working as engineers and especially surveyors. In the debates that took place around these issues the role of the handicrafts, and the artistic nature of architecture, were increasingly lost sight of. Architecture, to the institute, seemed to mean commerce. Many architects found their patience was running out and some formed a breakaway group to put pressure on the institute to help achieve their aims of legally closing the profession. Called The Society of Architects in 1891, they proposed a parliamentary bill to make this happen. Richard Norman Shaw, one of the leading architects of the day, saw red and, together with T.G. Jackson, met at the home of his former pupil Mervyn Macartney to plan a campaign of opposition.

Their tactics were to get the RIBA to oppose the Society of Architects' bill since it would surely need the support of the institute and its members to gain approval in Parliament. Shaw and Jackson drew up an open letter, or Memorial, to the institute which was published in *The Times* and signed by many of the leading artists of the day – who therefore became known as The Memorialists. Addressed 'To the President and Council of the Royal Institute of British Architects', the seventy signatories were divided into three camps – members of the institute (which included architects John Douglas [1830–1911], Arthur Blomfield [1829–99], Charles Hadfield [1840–1916], and J.J. Stevenson [1831–1908]), non-members of the institute (which if anything included even more impressive names drawn from the leading lights of the Gothic Revival, such as G.F. Bodley, William Butterfield, J.F. Bentley, Gilbert Scott, but also Webb, Lethaby and Mackmurdo, together with Jackson and Shaw), and finally those who weren't architects. This included the painters Alma-Tadema, John Brett, Ford Madox Brown, Hubert von Herkomer, Holman Hunt, Edward Burne-Jones, sculptors Stirling Lee

and Alfred Gilbert, and decorative artists such as Morris, Selwyn Image, Heywood Sumner and Walter Crane. It was an impressive list. Additionally, some members of the institute resigned their membership as part of their protest. It worked. The bill was delayed and registration and full legal closure was not achieved until the 1930s. The Memorialists had also written separately to the RIBA saying they wanted the institute to put forward its own, more acceptable bill, for a system of education, examination and registration that reflected the more artistic wing of the profession. It is salutary to note that at the end of a decade when they had achieved so much, the architect-craftsmen of the movement might have found themselves excluded from their profession. It is also interesting to reflect on the state of architecture at this moment in time, 1891, when the architectural profession seemed to be tearing itself apart and the Arts and Crafts Movement was in the ascendency.

## Avon Tyrrell

In the same year as the Memorialists were writing to *The Times*, a remarkable Arts and Crafts house, Avon Tyrrell, was also completed. Commissioned

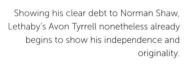

Showing his clear debt to Norman Shaw, Lethaby's Avon Tyrrell nonetheless already begins to show his independence and originality.

Avon Tyrrell's gables cut through the sky like a saw and the tall projecting bays play an interestingly off-centre game of counterpoint. Windows are clearly where they are needed for function not aesthetics and leave large areas of unpierced brickwork. The double-pitch of the roof allows the dormer windows of the servants' rooms to be set back discreetly from the main façade.

The gate out into the New Forest from the entrance court.

by Francis Henry, the first Lord Manners, this was the first building designed by Lethaby after leaving the office of Shaw. Although two of Shaw's other former staff, Ernest Newton and Mervyn Macartney, were also considered for the job, it is said that Shaw passed the job to Lethaby to help him establish his own independent practice. Known as a 'setting up' commission, Shaw did the same for many of his staff when they left him, Prior, for example, being given Carr Manor (1879–82) in Leeds.

Built on a magnificent site on the edge of the New Forest, Avon Tyrrell was paid for from the results of Lord Manners (when a young officer in the Grenadier Guards) making a bet in 1881 that he could buy, train and ride the winner of the Grand National of 1892! Astonishingly, and with no previous experience, he did just that and won £28,000 (roughly £3 million in today's money) as a result. At first sight there is little that is remarkable about the house. It demonstrates Lethaby's ten years working for Shaw as his chief assistant (in succession to Ernest Newton) with the servants' hall, kitchen and scullery externally expressed like one of Shaw's mature Queen Anne houses in Chelsea or Hampstead, with exposed red brick, deep white painted coving, a pitched roof held down by a picturesque flurry of chimney stacks and a mixture of vaguely seventeenth-century style windows. This connects to the main rooms of the house – its entrance hall, hall, drawing room, dining room and library. From the entrance courtyard this seems a somewhat inelegant mass of a building, possibly suggesting the form of a rather squat keep but that is probably to read too much into the design.

Its garden front is more conventional but also, according to Roderick Gradidge, it is here that this 'over-large' building sees Lethaby try 'to carry the cottage style into the field of the great house.'[52] This was to be a formal problem that beset the architects of the Arts and Crafts Movement, especially when building for the aristocracy. The garden front at Avon Tyrrell is long and straight and somewhat stiff, formal where cottage informality might be expected – its planar quality punctured by the projecting bays that run to the roof and light the first-floor bedrooms. These are then tied to the wall by a row of five counter-pointing triangular gables, which serve the nurseries and maids' rooms and, as Weaver commented, 'cut the sky like the teeth of a saw.'[53] Behind these hide smaller, barely noticeable dormers between the gables, which take advantage of the gambrel roof to recede into the background, leaving the garden front unaffected. To either end of this impressive façade the projecting hall bay and substantial chimney stack with its panels of not-quite chequerboard stone and brick panels act as heavy anchors or full stops to the lively design. Time and again it is this 'not quite' quality that impresses about Avon Tyrrell. Here for the first time is Lethaby, newly released from under Shaw's wing, a member of SPAB, an admirer of Webb, a founder member of the Art Workers' Guild, an enthusiastic exhibitor at the Arts and Crafts Exhibition Society, and a signatory of the Memorial opposed to the compulsory closure of the profession, putting the ideals

From afar what looks conventional, on closer inspection is anything but. Lethaby takes the idea of the Gothic finial and transposes it into the modern age as a realistically carved bouquet of roses to make innovation within tradition.

The running grapevine motif in the plasterwork was modelled by Lethaby's great friend Ernest Gimson, who collaborated with him on many other schemes.

Close-ups of two fireplaces reveal two approaches – realism depicting nature and realism of nature seen in the love of materials.

of the Arts and Crafts Movement into practice.

Gradidge has called the building 'doctrinaire'. Clearly the principle doctrine at work is to avoid historicism whilst honouring tradition. Hence the stone finial to the apex of the garden gate, from a distance suggesting something medieval or Gothic, on closer inspection is a garland of roses, tied together with a piece of string. Similar ahistorical rope motifs also run around the gate piers of the carriage entrance and are found to the retaining walls of the garden terrace. Internally all the plasterwork was designed and modelled by his great friend Gimson, and depicts vines, flowers, apples, pears and similar motifs drawn from nature without any hint of historicism. The same motifs, drawn freshly from nature, can be found in the wood carving to the staircase and the carving to the alabaster in the drawing room fireplace.

By the time the building was completed, Lethaby had written two important books that established first his originality and then his scholarship. First was *Architecture, Mysticism, and Myth* in 1891. This laid the basis for the symbolism inherent in the English Free Style that Lethaby came to champion. Then, in 1894 (with his friend Harold Swainson), and partly as a repost to what he himself saw as the 'amateur' nature of his first book, was a comprehensive account of one of the great buildings of Western Christianity, *The Church of Sancta Sophia, Constantinople; A study of Byzantine building*. The influence of both these

books can be seen in Avon Tyrrell. Symbolism is found in its claim to be a 'calendar house' having 365 windows, fifty-two rooms, twelve chimneys, seven ground floor entrances, and four floors – in other words the house symbolizes respectively the days, weeks, and months of the year, then the days of the week, and the seasons of the year. Other conceits – geometrical and decorative – can be found in relation to Lethaby's first book. More influential perhaps is the 'study of Byzantine building'. This manifests itself most tellingly in the tour de force of the fireplaces in Avon Tyrrell. Coloured marbles are a particular feature of Byzantine architecture and one Lethaby and Swainson were at pains to discuss in their book. Here he delights in choosing different marbles for different

One of Lethaby's most daring fireplaces delights in the use of pattern and material selection for its effect. Gimson's plasterwork is just visible above.

rooms and then letting the material speak for itself, as Weaver commented, '... the beauty of large, smooth, coloured surfaces, patterned on lines of fresh severity'. Elsewhere in the house this 'unaffected' approach to the detail – its panelling, plasterwork, ironwork and so on – goes out of its way to avoid being able to be categorized in an archaeologically accurate sense.

Avon Tyrrell is a triumph of Arts and Craft principles in its delight in craftsmanship and tradition but without copying the past, and it is hard to disagree with Weaver's conclusion that it '... shows how originality, working within defined limits, may produce stimulating results by re-arranging elements which have gone to build up the architecture of the past'. It shows architecture as the art the Memorialists fervently believed it to be in 1891and not a slave to commerce or copying the past. Lethaby should have the last word. At the end of his first book he asked, 'What, then, will this art of the future be? The message will still be of nature and man, of order and beauty, but it will be sweetness, simplicity, freedom, confidence and light.'[54]

The bold composition of Standen includes making the water tower suggest a medieval keep buried deep in the building's history. Arts and Crafts architects enjoyed playing with such archetypes once stripped of their historic detail.

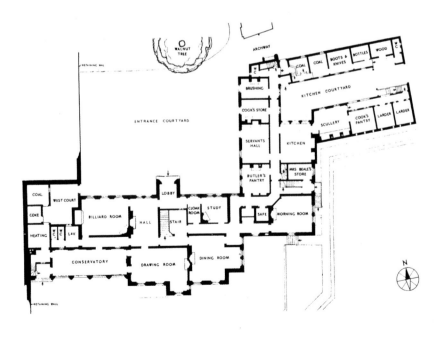

After the Red House, Standen, near East Grinstead in leafy Sussex, is probably Webb's best-known house. With stunning views over the Ashdown Forest and the Medway Valley beyond, it was built for a prosperous London solicitor, James Samuel Beale (1840–1912). Construction began in July 1892 and the family moved in two years later in August 1894 – so it is broadly contemporary with Avon Tyrrell. Both externally, and especially internally, it displays a strong taste for the Arts and Crafts and given the date of construction this also included electric light – the light fittings being designed by Benson with its opalescent glass shades being manufactured by Powell's of Whitefriars.

James was the son of a powerful Birmingham Unitarian dynasty, which had made its money through the growth of the railways, and especially the success of the Midland Railway Company. His uncle, Samuel, was mayor in 1841, whilst his brothers included Charles, a three-times mayor, and William, a notable barrister involved in the powerful Liberal Party which came to dominate Birmingham. As the Midland Railway prospered and opened their magnificent new terminus and associated hotel at St Pancras in London, so the firm of Beale & Co. opened an office in the capital with James in charge in the 1870s. Initially they lived in fashionable Holland Park, rubbing shoulders with the Anglo-Greek

Rather than demolish, Webb urged his clients to keep this typical Sussex cottage, Hollybush Farm, and incorporate it into the new house as part of the service wing.

Alexander and Constantine Ionides (notable early patrons of Morris & Co.) possessed of several fine Arts and Crafts houses, including Webb's No. 1, Palace Green. This was the house originally built for the Howard family that so baffled Webb's contemporaries by its apparent lack of a recognizable style. At Standen, he takes this principle even further.

From 1884, and the opening of a new branch line from Oxted to East Grinstead, many new houses began to be built in this part of the county – often for relaxation and holidays rather than as main homes. Beale soon realized he was able to commute from East Grinstead to London and in 1890 bought some land. It included two old farms, Hollybush and Stone farm. Surely being aware of Webb's work in Holland Park (to which it

has some affinities) and elsewhere, he approached him to design the new house. Courtesy of an extensive set of documents we have a very clear picture of the development of the design. Webb recorded in his account book for 20 March 1891, 'Mr Beale first called here to ask me to advise him, and design a house etc for Hollybush Farm'.[55] The first visit took place on 11 April 1891 and before long Webb had persuaded his clients to both site the house in a more sheltered position than they had considered and, as at Forthampton, to incorporate, rather than demolish, some of the existing buildings, one of which dated back to the mid-fifteenth century. This was of course not only pragmatic but followed the ethos of SPAB.

Webb delighted in the inherent beauty of local materials at Standen and instructed that it be built with 'the best materials and workmanship'.

Together, these two buildings, Hollybush Farm and its barn, suggested not only the north and west sides of the building but also the scale and materiality of its new service wing, which grows seamlessly out of it by the device of an archway, or agricultural drift-way – hung tiles in a fish-scale pattern, local Horsham stone roof slates, and small-paned casement windows. Webb followed the colours, textures, and local charac-ter found here in his thinking about the new house – only the limited use of roughcast for practical

reasons departed from the precise local vernacular tradition.

On 7 November 1891 Webb pegged out the building on the ground to check the dimensions and began working up detailed drawings so that by June 1892 he was able to issue specifications. This included the general instruction that, 'The whole of the work is to be done with the best materials and work-manship of their several kinds . . .' This included stone quarried from the site (now a garden), which Webb instructed more particularly

should be dressed to resemble that '. . . of the kind shown in some old walling at the back of The Ship Inn, East Grinstead.' For its brick, Webb had learned from his first 'statement' building at Upton and leavened the red Keymer brick by specifying a local yellow-grey brick from Horsham, leaving the red to be used only for dressing doors and windows and so on. Similarly, when he came to specify the hung-tile work he didn't seek to replicate the fish-scale pattern of Hollybush but contrasted it with plainer clay tiles which, being hand-made, would be

The layering of materials – stone, brick, timber and tile – is seen at its best in this section of the garden front.

and timber. This projects from a larger body of the house to the rear (containing twelve bedrooms, one bathroom, and two lavatories) denoted by lime-washed rough-cast and a large unbroken clay-tiled roof. Five irregularly placed, large, elongated brick chimney stacks seem to stake the building to the ground and an additional strong anchor and contrast to the buildings horizontality is provided by the tower element (a water tower), as if the remainder of a small medieval tower keep but here fancifully topped off by a bel-vedere and crisp railings to enclose a viewing platform. To the west of

in a variety of shades and colours. Working closely with his clients during this work, Webb for example designed built-in furniture in the bedroom and dressing room for the Beales' eldest daughter, Amy, following discussions with her in August 1893.

At the Red House, Webb's even use of red brick had belied his attempts to suggest a building that had grown over the centuries. Here at Standen, thirty years later, Webb has developed his approach and mastered the use of materials as the specification demonstrates. From the south, or garden front, the varied use of materials, attached to powerfully evocative forms, suggests various phases of building. The grid-like rational five-gabled weather-boarded front is layered by its materials from ground to gable – stone, hung-tile,

The service wing connects with the old cottage – its large weather-boarded gables look back to Webb's earlier house, Joldwynds.

Large new mullion and transomed windows were introduced after the house was finished to lighten the entrance hall.

this principle elevation is an almost informal conservatory, but given some stature by the inclusion of a smaller belvedere to balance the high level one on top of the tower. Constructionally its exposed metal trusses hark back to Webb's work for the Bell family of iron-founders, one of his most loyal clients, in their Middlesbrough offices, which he designed in 1883.

In the entrance courtyard the tower dominates whilst the weather-boarded gables are larger to the service wing and hark back to Joldwynds (1874) and Coneyhurst

(1886), and the main body of the house is more apparent being unimpeded by the projections on the garden front. Once completed the original entrance hall – as ever harking back to the medieval hall – was found to be too dark, doubtless not helped by being painted in Webb's favourite dragon's blood red, so four years after completion in 1898, Webb was commissioned to refashion it by the inclusion of a new eight-light mullioned window and also made minor changes to the conservatory corridor and billiard room fireplace. Showing how SPAB principles influenced his

thinking, the new entrance hall was carried out in stone to distinguish it from the older version, even though only four years older. It was the honest thing to do.

One of Webb's tests of his work was that, 'I never begin to be satisfied until my work looks commonplace'. Overall the varied outline and massing, extension and modification of the materials and forms of the older buildings, and invention, mark Standen out as one of the finest buildings of the Arts and Crafts Movement – commonplace or not.

# Chapter 4

# Building on a Secure Foundation – the 'Sons of Shaw'

Robert Weir Schultz's perspective of a house near Edenbridge, taken from W. Shaw Sparrow's *The Modern Home* (1906), is one of several exploiting the idea of the butterfly plan around this time.

WITH SPAB, THE VARIOUS GUILDS AND the Exhibition Society up and running, and a sense of unity and purpose provided by the fight against registration, by the early 1890s the architect members of these key organizations began to put into practice the concepts that underpinned their work and created a network of common values they all shared.

It is remarkable how few offices, all London-based, these young architects came from. Chief amongst them were those of Sedding, Ernest George & Peto, but most of all Richard Norman Shaw. Shaw had taken over from Webb as Street's chief assistant in 1859, just before Morris left. Most of Shaw's pupils and assistants retained a strong affection for the amiable Scot and his office and referred to it as 'the

Opposite: Metal is plaited like rope to form this door-hinge at All Saints', Brockhampton.

family'. That being so it is appropriate to think of this talented generation of young architects who formed the backbone of the Arts and Crafts Movement as 'the sons of Shaw'. They were a tight-knit bunch who came to prominence in the 1880s, and then dominated the progressive architecture of the 1890s and early 1900s. Looking to Webb as a guiding spirit, their work forms the high point of the architecture of the Arts and Crafts Movement – at its best daring, original, style-less. Many went on to develop successful careers working safely within the recognizable historical styles popular at the time such as the Early Renaissance, Neo-Georgian, Tudor and especially the Domestic Revival. Many continued to debate Arts and Crafts concerns and stayed active members of the guild, exhibited at the Exhibition Society but also embraced the Royal Academy and the RIBA. Architects such as Reginald Blomfield developed a country house practice with 'Wrenaissance' style buildings, for example Moundsmere Manor (1908); Ernest Newton carefully refurbished Bullers Wood in a Shavian manner in 1889 but eventually 'gave way' to Neo-Georgian; Mervyn Macartney embraced, as the title of one of his many publications called it, 'Later Renaissance Architecture in England' as can be seen in houses such as Kennet Orley (1905), whilst Robert Schultz Weir continued to plough the vernacular furrow for much of his life with buildings such as How Green (1907), as did Sidney Barnsley in various buildings in and around Painswick. However, two of Shaw's staff stand out in particular for advancing the ideals of the movement – Lethaby and Prior.

## W.R. Lethaby

Usually referred to as W.R. Lethaby (rather than William), this shy young Devonian was the most gifted of Shaw's students, especially considering his origins and background. This was not only the judgement of future generations but also of Shaw himself. According to Robert Schultz Weir, when someone referred to Lethaby as one of Shaw's pupils he corrected him by saying, '. . . on the contrary it is I who am Lethaby's pupil'.[56] Despite this, the artistic debt Lethaby owes to Shaw is very clear in his early domestic work such as Avon Tyrrell, Melsetter House, The

Hurst, and High Coxlease – all Shavian in their clear planning, but with an increasing nod to Webb whose biography he was to write, and who, like so many, he first met through the meetings of SPAB.

### Early life and career

Part of Lethaby's particular character and approach to architecture may be gleaned from his background. Born in 1857 in the Devon market town of Barnstaple, his father was a carver and gilder of picture frames so Lethaby was born into the handicrafts. For all that, it does not seem to have been a joyous household. His parents were Bible Christians, a particularly austere form of the Non-Conformist faith that left a major, largely adverse, legacy to Lethaby. It is ironic that one of the great architect-scholars of the Arts and Crafts Movement, and one who built part of his reputation on understanding Christian architecture, and received the considerable accolade of being appointed the Surveyor to the Fabric of Westminster Abbey, should have had little time for organized religion as he grew up as a result of his upbringing. His American wife, Edith, was clearly hurt by Lethaby's refusal to accompany her to church on Sunday mornings when he would prefer to stay in bed, and confided in a friend that she always hoped he would change his mind. Personal fulfilment

Now demolished, Lethaby's house, The Hurst, on the Four Oaks estate in Sutton Coldfield was a unique excursion into Georgian architecture. (Lawrence Weaver, *Small Country Houses of To-day* 1922)

and joy came through creativity for Lethaby – as he had carved on his gravestone in Hartley Witney – 'Love and Labour are all'.

Writing a leaflet on designing games for the Dryad furniture and handicrafts company of Leicester – founded by his friend Harry Peach (1874–1936) – Lethaby recalled in 1929 that had it not been for a neighbour in Barnstaple who would entertain him by making simple paper animals he might never have had this creativity unlocked. It is interesting to note the parallels of this story on the importance of play in children's development to that of the upbringing of the great American architect, Frank Lloyd Wright, and the professed impact that Froebel toy building blocks had on him.

After serving his articles from 1871 in the office of local painter turned architect Alexander Lauder in Barnstaple, he stayed as his assistant until 1878. Lauder must have been an ideal teacher for any future member of the Arts and Crafts Movement. Many years later Lauder's grandson recalled that he '. . . would decorate many of the houses he built with huge sgraffito murals, terracotta friezes and high relief ceramic tiles, all carved and modelled with his own hand… he used to insist that all the men working on his own buildings should have an understanding of one another's craft, so that each might feel that he was building a house and not just practicing carpentry, bricklaying or plumbing.'[57] After leaving Barnstaple, Lethaby spent a year travelling the country, briefly working in other architects' offices in Derbyshire, and then Leicester, to gain wider experience.

## From the provinces to London

Clearly ambitious, at the same time he was also submitting work to designing competitions in magazines such as *The Building News*. It was one of these that, in 1879, brought him to the attention of Shaw, who appointed him as his new chief assistant to take over from Ernest Newton. With his artisan background,

the humble twenty-one-year-old Lethaby would have stood out from the predominantly upper-middle class, confident, public school- and university-educated pupils and assistants of Shaw. Quickly, not only his talent but also his sense of fun endeared him to all. Former pupils recall Shaw and Lethaby deciding to hold an impromptu cricket match in the office one dull afternoon, substituting rulers and rubbers for bat and ball.

The ten years that Lethaby was in Shaw's office were the years when the master was working on major commissions such as Cragside (1869–82) for the armaments manufacturer William Armstrong (1810–90), New Scotland Yard for the Metropolitan Police (1888–90), and minor commissions such as All Saints' (1885–87), Leek, Staffordshire. His recognition of the place of historic precedent in the creation of a new architecture was well expressed by his use of the expression, 'Would you know the new, you must search the old.'[58] Lethaby's ability as a draughtsman, quite apart from his understanding of historical architecture, is evident in the drawings for such works as the giant marble Renaissance fireplace in the drawing room at Cragside. It was this draughting ability that in 1879 had won him the prestigious Soane Medallion and Travelling Scholarship, which he used to travel to France where he sketched and measured nearly thirty cathedrals. But Lethaby was clearly much more than an accomplished and competent draughtsman who was content to work within the confines of historicism – if that was all he was, it's questionable if so inventive an architect as Shaw would have employed him. Projects for Shaw, such as the brooding black marble font at Leek, look forward to Lethaby the symbolist, whose first book *Architecture, Mysticism and Myth* published in 1891 sought to find a way out of the cul-de-sac of revivalism.

Once catapulted into the life of the capital city, Lethaby lost no time in extending his education by attending the prestigious evening classes at the Royal Academy and supplementing this with spare time spent studying the collections of the British Museum and Victoria and Albert Museum. Immersing himself

Exhibited at the Arts and Crafts Exhibition Society, this altar frontal is decorated in gesso by Lethaby. (Courtesy of Ian Johnson)

other members of 'the family' – Reginald Blomfield, Mervyn Macartney and Sidney Barnsley – then established the short-lived furniture company, Kenton & Co. (1890–92) in a converted stable (near Kenton Street), employing five professional cabinet-makers to execute their designs. Despite its failure, Lethaby continued to design a variety of decorative goods for Morris & Co. and others as a means to supplement his income and demonstrate the 'unity of the arts' with the architect working as a craftsman. So auspicious a start to a career would suggest great professional success lay ahead – and so it did, but not as an architect. Although acclaimed, Lethaby only completed six buildings during his working life. But as Muthesius recognized, 'The number of his houses is not large, but all appear to be masterpieces.'

## The move to education

From 1896 when, together with the sculptor George Frampton (1868–1928), he was appointed the joint director of the new Central School of Arts and Crafts in London, his life was largely given over to education and writing as a means of promoting the core of his deeply held beliefs on the unity of all the arts. At Central he gathered around him all the skilled artist-craftsmen of his day including his fellow guildsman, Halsey Ricardo (1854–1928), who became Central's first teacher of architecture. Here Lethaby implemented ideas he outlined later in *The Architectural Review* on architectural education that, 'The highly artificial separation of the present system is obviously disastrous to progress in building . . . all who are to be engaged in building in any skilled capacity should meet in schools common to all.'[59] It was this system of education – which brought all the skills needed to create buildings together to be taught side-by-side and established at Central – that was emulated later by the Deutsche Werkbund in Germany in bringing together art and industry, and most famously with Walter Gropius in establishing the Bauhaus in Germany in 1919. In 1910 in a letter

in such a stimulating environment, it is little wonder that in early 1883, Lethaby became one of the founders of the St George's Art Society. Neither is it a surprise that he became a key member of the Art Workers' Guild (becoming its Master in 1911), SPAB, the Arts and Crafts Exhibition Society, and was a vociferous opponent of registration. With the society he exhibited various designs over the years for chairs, embroidery, metal work, and particularly fireplaces for manufacturers such as Farmer & Brindley, Longden & Co., and the Coalbrookdale Company. In 1889 he exhibited the gesso altar frontal designed for Prior's innovative church at Bothenhampton. It seems to display some of the craft skills he had surely acquired from his father as gesso is one of the essential skills of the frame-maker. His friend and collaborator Gimson, who first took him to a SPAB meeting, praised his furniture as 'wonderful furniture of a commonplace kind'. Together with Gimson, he and to Lethaby, Gimson claimed that, 'After all it seems to have been our Craft Eden that made possible the German Werkbund.'[60]

Further accolades followed, including being appointed to be the first Professor of Ornament and Design at the Royal College of Art in 1900. Just as at Central, he began to infiltrate the school with Arts and Crafts devotees such as his close friend and ally, Arthur Beresford Pite (1861–1934), who was appointed Professor of Architecture in 1900. Of course, this additional appointment (he kept both positions for a while) took Lethaby still further away from practising as an architect – a fact which Roderick Gradidge has claimed is responsible for making him 'doctrinaire'. Gradidge found his buildings too theoretical as he developed, and labelled some elements as 'cranky'.

## 'The number of his houses is not large . . .'

His first independent commission, Avon Tyrrell was, as we have seen in the previous chapter, an uncompromising attempt to put Arts and Crafts naturalist principles in decoration into practice. It led to other country houses and reflects the fact that, despite the appeal of both symbolism and then Byzantine architecture, as he later recalled, 'The happy chance of close intimacy with Philip Webb at last satisfied my mind about that mysterious thing we call "Architecture". From him I learnt that what I was going to mean by architecture was not mere designs, forms and grandeurs, but *buildings*, honest and human, with hearts in them.'[61] This meant more than the happy coincidence of the gables at Avon Tyrrell strongly recalling Webb's at Standen, but always going back to first principles in design rather than copying the past.

Lethaby almost worshipped Webb and in so many ways is the conduit through which Webb's influence was developed. In his biography of the older man he stated that, 'I write not because I can judge Philip Webb but rather that in his life I find a means of judging my own', and concluded that, 'My subject as I see it is the architect as hero.'[62] Lethaby's other

country houses – Melsetter, The Hurst, and High Coxlease – are not the best places to see Webb's influence but rather the astonishingly original Eagle Insurance Company building (1900), Colmore Row, Birmingham and All Saints' Church (1902), Brockhampton, near Ross-on-Wye.

## Lethaby in town and country

At the Eagle Insurance Building, Lethaby, working with the Birmingham architect J.L. Ball (1852–1933), designed an office building without any overt reference to previous historic styles. The large grid of the transom and mullioned window seems to grow out

The Eagle Assurance building in Birmingham is Lethaby's only urban building and begins to show what happens when the Arts and Crafts came into town – cottages and manor houses just don't work anymore. (Licensed under the Creative Commons Attribution 2.0 Generic license. © Tony Hisgett)

of the pavement the building sits on and floods the ground floor with light. The entrances either side – with bright polished bronze doors containing shining circular motifs – relate to Lethaby's ideas on symbolism to represent sun-gateways, whilst the coincidence of the company's name allows a carved eagle to be flying through discs representing planets on the parapet. Between this 'ceiling like the sky', and the 'entrances for the sun and moon', is a further three floors linked by a large sparse grid of windows. The Eagle Insurance Building is one of those buildings singled out by Nikolaus Pevsner in a perceptive article, *Nine Swallows – No Summer*, where he sees the building as of such originality that it was seen as a harbinger of the new approach to architecture of the twentieth century. It represents more ably than any other building what happened to the Arts and Crafts country-cottage idiom when confronted with urban, not rural, life – commerce, not agriculture.

In contrast, Brockhampton in Herefordshire is very rural. Yet Lethaby's design is no less compromising than that of the Eagle Insurance Company. All Saints', considered in more detail at the end of this chapter, is uncompromising with its unusual construction that used a traditional thatch to cover a concrete roof, supported on transverse arches that almost sweep down to the church floor. Had Lethaby's group entry for the Byzantinist Liverpool Cathedral competition in 1902 – submitted under Henry Wilson's name – and even more, the joint design he was invited to submit for Letchworth Garden City with Halsey Ricardo – been successful, Lethaby would be recognized as a major architect of the movement more than his small handful of buildings allow. That reputation falls to his friend Edward Prior.

## Edward Schroder Prior

Prior's background couldn't have been more different from Lethaby's and was in many ways more typical of a Victorian architect. Born in Greenwich, his father was a barrister who died when Edward was only three years old in a horse-riding accident. Nonetheless his resolute mother moved the family to Harrow to ensure he could attend a good school and where she could be on hand. Here he did well in athletics, the classics, and natural history – becoming an avid collector of butterflies. A devout Anglican and a High Tory, thirty years after he left the school (by which time he was not only a successful architect but also a well-respected scholar of medieval architecture) he sent a copy of one of his books to the school library where he said he'd read Ruskin and '... first thought upon art'.[63] After a promising start at Cambridge University reading Classics – an education he later observed hadn't equipped him to be an architect – he accepted that it was due to his growing interest in architecture, and cycling around Cambridgeshire sketching old buildings, that led to his receiving only a third-class honours degree. Despite his poor performance, after graduation he entered Shaw's office as an articled pupil in 1874. He was thus around at the very start of Shaw's development of the Queen Anne style, his work for Jonathan Carr at Bedford Park, and when Ernest Newton was still Shaw's chief clerk. By the time Lethaby arrived five years later, Prior was all but ready to leave, the two men barely overlapping. A quixotic character, although he was a founder member of both the Art Workers' Guild and the Arts and Crafts Exhibition Society, he never joined SPAB, became an associate of the Royal Academy, and seems to have thought of Lethaby's revered Webb more as a shrewd businessman than a progressive architect-craftsman.

Despite these differences, to the majority of the Arts and Crafts Movement he was always regarded as the most original and inventive of them – Shaw called him '... perhaps the most gifted pupil of them all'[64] – but this inventiveness could as readily as not be seen as eccentric and idiosyncratic. A staunch individualist (Reginald Blomfield reckoned that '... he enjoyed being in a majority of one'), unlike other pupils of Shaw's he seems content to have received his training from Shaw without supplementing it with classes at the Royal Academy, Architectural Association, or any other institutions that catered for architectural education beyond the confines of the office. Critical of his own drawing ability (the cost of drawing classes at Harrow had been beyond his family's means), he took refuge in making models and if his builders lacked detailed drawings, then so much the better as far as he was concerned as this allowed for a freer and looser process of design and construction more akin to medieval methods. Like many Arts and Crafts architects, once he set up on his own he kept a very small office (just one or two assistants) so he could keep control of jobs and do much of the work himself – leaving site supervision to one of his assistants.

## Independent practice

When he left Shaw's office in 1879, Shaw passed on his usual setting-up commission for his more talented pupils. This was Carr Manor (1879–82), on the outskirts of Leeds, for the local physician Dr Thomas Allbutt. A large house dominated by five gables, it was a reworking of the original late seventeenth-century house on the site. Only its extensive use of the dark local Horsforth gritstone differentiates it from the kind of house Shaw was designing for such clients at the time. Elsewhere in the early 1880s – as at High Grove, Eastcote (1880–81) and Manor Lodge, Harrow-on-the-Hill (1884) – Prior shows himself every inch the pupil

of Shaw. Over half of his commissions were houses and many were the result of family, school or university connections emanating out of Dorset, Harrow or Cambridge. His mother, like his future wife, came from Bridport in Dorset and it was there, perhaps due to the liberty he felt he had as a result of these family connections, that he began to branch out as an architect of power and originality and shake off Shaw's mantel.

## 'Go west young man . . .'

Holy Trinity Church, Bothenhampton (1884–89) is close to Bridport, and closer still to Symondsbury from where Prior's wife – the local vicar's daughter – hailed from. At first sight it resembles a small conventional parish church in a revived Early English style, built of the local stone. True, there is something a little unsettling about the way the nave buttresses puncture the eaves, waving their elegant coping stones against the large pitched roof. Unsettling also is the corbelling of the small bell-cote (one of Prior's earlier designs gave the church a small transverse tower). However, this slight sense of unease fails to prepare the visitor for the powerfully primitive and uninterrupted interior space where the roof is held up by four transverse masonry arches which sweep down low to the floor like great wishbones – the ribs that

Holy Trinity, Bothenhampton. (Courtesy of Ian Johnson)

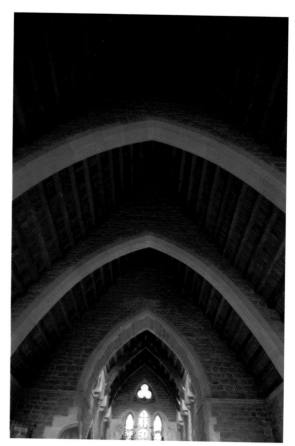

The experimental nature of the transverse arch construction led to long delays before approval was given. (Courtesy of Ian Johnson)

necessitate those large buttresses either side.

Designed a good decade before Lethaby's similar concept for the roof of All Saints', Brockhampton, and even longer before Prior's best-known church masterpiece, St Andrew's, Roker (1904–07), Bothenhampton's roof seems to anticipate both whilst also exemplifying his analysis of medieval architecture that '. . . the art of the medieval ages was not this architectural dress, but something underneath it.'[65] The effect is to create a secure, cave-like, primitive feel to the interior. Originally designed in 1884, construction did not begin until 1887 as the Incorporated Church Building Society, who were part funding the new church, were unconvinced of the structural safety of the radical roof design. Finally completed in 1889, Prior is reputed to have partly funded the work himself due to his dismay at the

delay his inventiveness caused. In any case it seems he supplied the altar rails, altar table and frontal, the latter designed by Lethaby.

## Gone fishing . . .

Prior's design for Pier Terrace, West Bay, Bridport is a further step away from Shaw and clearly relates to his developing ideas on the textural quality of architecture. Originally called Quay Terrace, it was designed between 1884 and 1885. It is both the design and the function of the building that excites. We have the Great Western Railway to thank for it. The construction of a new railway line to Bridport in 1857 led to the decline of its harbour and this was subsequently refashioned as the seaside resort of West Bay with the arrival of a branch line in 1883. Prior's family connections were clearly helpful as two of his cousins were directors of the West Bay Building Company, which was developing the new resort. Incidentally one of them, J.P.F. Grundy, was also one of the promoters of the new church at Bothenhampton. It was as the church was being constructed in 1885 that Prior married Louisa Maunsell, the daughter of the vicar of nearby Symondsbury church (where Lethaby designed a stained-glass window, as he had probably done for Bothenhampton).

Prior's initial design for West Bay was ambitious – hotel, cottages, boarding houses, swimming pool with shops, a tea room, and a club house all set out on a new promenade – an enormous undertaking. However, one of the two principle landowners was the famous archaeologist General Augustus Pitt-Rivers (1827–1900). He refused to release sufficient land for the development so it was back to the drawing board and the Harbour Commissioners were approached with a different design. Overlooking the harbour, Prior's long, tall, cliff-like terrace of ten boarding houses provided sixty bedrooms for holidaymakers. The individual house units are barely noticeable and as they give way to the general character of the block, which is surely without precedent as a building

When constructed in 1884, Pier Terrace in West Bay was a novel new building type to cater for the expansion of tourism – a purpose-built boarding house for the middle class, arranged as a large terrace overlooking the harbour.

type, perhaps only Blackpool at this date was starting to develop purpose-designed boarding houses for holiday resorts, and these were of a very different character aimed at a working-class customer. Each house has a half-basement containing a kitchen, scullery and living room for the landlady and her family. Guests were given a living room and two bedrooms to the first floor with a further living room, bedroom and toilet to the second floor. To the odd Mansard roof with its ingenious dormer windows tucked under the continuous hip, the attic provided three further bedrooms – one large and two small.

Beyond the functional requirements of the terrace, Prior's artistry recasts the relatively new typology of the boarding house as a geological slice of the local landscape. Set at right angles to the nearby cliff face, Prior takes the particular textures, colours and forms of the local landscape as the inspiration for his design. Whilst it provides unity – from the starting point of Portland stone as it comes out of the ground, through to hung slate, roughcast, and clay tiles – it does so by deploying these disparate materials as if geological layers, the overhanging Mansard roof and

Prior's design layers the materials like the geological strata of the nearby cliffs.

projecting bay windows mirroring stone outcrops in the undulatingly eroded cliff. His elevation drawing of 1884 clearly shows his thinking with its three layers of colour wash, demonstrating, as he wrote, 'At a still further distance the larger architectural features themselves – such as windows and piers, pinnacles and buttresses – merge into an undistinguished variegation of surface.'[66] Texture is clearly a major motif in his work as shown here and develops more clearly in The Barn in Exmouth, and Voewood at High Kelling, Norfolk.

Pier Terrace is Prior's first attempt to connect with geology in this way and was designed in advance of his major written statement on this approach. This was 'Texture as a Quality of Art and a Condition for Architecture', which he delivered in 1889 at a meeting of the National Association for the Advancement of Art and its application to industry in Edinburgh. Part of the section of the conference devoted to 'Painting, Sculpture and Applied Art', it was chaired by William Morris. Founded in 1887, this was only this influential body's second conference '… to discuss problems of a practical nature connected with the welfare of the Arts, Fine and Applied.' Mackmurdo was very much its champion and may have joined the Art Workers' Guild in 1888 only to drum up support for this second congress. Other guildsmen, such as

Sedding and Ashbee, also attended and Walter Crane noted approvingly in his *Reminiscences* that, 'The Arts and Crafts banner was well to the fore, and the movement made way all along the line as the most practical effort to unite Art and Industry.'[67]

Just as with Lethaby's first publication, *Architecture, Mysticism, and Myth*, which despite its obscure references can be seen as holding the germ of so much of his architectural development, so it is with this first published lecture by Prior. Both men effectively set out their architectural ideas before developing as the scholars of medieval architecture they were subsequently remembered as for much of their architectural careers.

## 'The texture of architecture'

The finest realization of this textual approach can be seen in his two best-known houses – The Barn, Exmouth and Voewood, High Kelling, Norfolk. The Barn, an interesting name in itself, is the building that gave Prior most public acclaim following its recognition by Hermann Muthesius in *Das Englische Haus* (1904–05). Here it is simply referred to as '. . . the house with the remarkable plan.'[68] This was Prior's use of what is known as the butterfly plan. It

The Barn is the most celebrated butterfly-plan house in the country – its original thatched roof has been replaced by tiles after it was destroyed by fire. (Courtesy of The Beach House, Exmouth)

so impressed Muthesius that he used it at his own house, Freudenberg (1907–08), in Berlin. Why it is called The Barn is hard to understand beyond its vernacular character. This used to be more apparent before the roof was slated following a fire that destroyed the original thatch – and much else. Maybe it can be viewed as looking like a conversion of an earlier agricultural building given the way the gables sit on the roof as if they had been inserted at a later date – a reading reinforced by the presence of a very self-consciously Serlian window – but executed in a vernacular manner – set in the only smooth ashlar on the building, to the front staircase. But for all his eccentricities, and admiration for George Devey (who delighted in 'faking it'), Prior didn't usually play this sort of game with his buildings, which Devey did so readily.

The design originated in a clay model submitted to the Royal Academy for its 1895 exhibition. Architectural models were rare so this was a radical submission and so it is perhaps all the more startling that the Academy accepted it. The reviewer in *The Builder* welcomed it enthusiastically and noted that, 'It is comparatively rough in its appearance and revolutionary in its tendencies', and, given the 'Profession or Art' debate, went on to comment that, 'We do not like to suggest anything so much below the dignity of "professional" architecture but we strongly suspect Mr Prior of having made the model with his own hands. He is quite capable of it.'[69] Whether he made this one or not we don't know but – given the roughness – on the balance of probability the reviewer is right. We do know that his next-door neighbour in London's St John's Wood, the architect Charles Voysey, enjoyed helping him make models and Prior exhibited a more ambitious one of a courtyard house four years later at the 1899 exhibition. It seems for architects of the Arts and Crafts persuasion, models were an acceptable form of submission to exhibitions rather than the highly accomplished watercolour perspectives of mainstream established architects, or more often specialist artists employed to make their designs more attractive to potential clients.

The house was commissioned by a friend of Prior's from Harrow, Major Henry Wetherall, and house and garden are an integrated design. Prior wrote that, 'Its enclosing walls, 9ft high and thatched for coping, will give shade; its angles provide arbours and shelter from every wind, so that hour by hour, and day after day, there can always be ease and delight in it and never monotony as the seasons come and go and cloud and sunshine alternate.'[70] The plan of the house, looking like a butterfly, was not without precedent but was nonetheless unusual. The French architect, Eugène Viollet-le-Duc (1814–79), had illustrated one in 1864 and we know that Shaw recommended that his students study the works of this great structural rationalist. Perhaps the Frenchman even influenced Shaw's own work as his remodelling of the eighteenth-century house, Chesters, in 1891 – where he added five wings to the original core of the house – is often cited as another possible source for Prior's radical plan.

The point of a butterfly plan, as its alternative name of double suntrap house suggests, is to catch the maximum amount of light and heat. It is a wholly functional response to the environment but which, by placing two or more wings radiating out from a central core of a building, causes a few internal difficulties such as odd triangular corners where wings connect to the core. The usual response to this, as Prior did both here and at Voewood (his most spectacular butterfly-plan house built a decade later) was to use these oddly shaped corners for staircases. It is also a good example of what the Arts and Crafts Movement increasingly came to view as rational design. What butterfly houses lack in an expansive and dignified staircase they make up for by magnificent central halls, sun-filled vistas, airy rooms, and a varied roofscape. Given the Arts and Crafts Movement's socialist credentials, butterfly plans also destroyed the usual hierarchy of a house where the servants' wing is of an inferior architectural quality to that of the rest of the house such as, for example, Avon Tyrrell. But Prior was no socialist.

As built, The Barn had subtle changes from the

Whilst the peculiar chimney stacks of The Barn aren't local, the building materials certainly are!

textural effect with large beach pebbles to connect with the local vernacular. However, much of this is facing material, the walls being constructed of concrete and ballast from the excavations to form the sunken garden to the south and with complete tree trunks as reinforcement. Clearly Prior had reached a point in his career where textural effect and its power to suggest geology, more than honesty, was his architectural master.

The Barn was the instigator of several other significant butterfly houses over the next few decades, perhaps the most unexpected being the modest gardener's house in Steep, probably designed by Alfred Powell. This otherwise unassuming design is timber framed, with a tile-hung roof so low that gutters are fixed at waist height, and the internal walls slope inwards, making the hanging of pictures somewhat difficult. Others include Happisburgh Manor, Happisburgh, Norfolk, by Detmar Blow to a design by Ernest Gimson (1900); Papillon Hall, Lubenham, Leicestershire, by Edwin Lutyens (1902–4, demolished in 1950); Kelling Hall, Kelling, Norfolk (1913) and Yaffle Hill, Broadstone, Dorset (1930), both by Edward Maufe; but most of all Prior's masterpiece, Voewood.

model of 1895 whilst retaining the unusual planform. Most obvious was replacing the tiled roof for thatch and replacing the three rather conventional chimney stacks with two great circular stacks of a vernacular pattern mainly found in the Lake District. They seem almost like giant handles on a model of the building, allowing the wings of the house to be moved back and forth. This apparent departure from basing the building in its locality is a tension elsewhere in The Barn but also a large part of its originality. Outwardly its walls seem built of local stone, interspersed for

Row Cottage, Steep, built by Geoffrey Lupton, possibly designed by Alfred Powell – a small butterfly-plan house of timber-framed construction, the walls slope inside, making the hanging of pictures rather difficult.

Voewood – surely one of the most inventive, original and somewhat eccentric buildings of its day. It delights in texture, one of Edward Prior's great interests. (© Martin Godfrey Cook)

## Voewood – 'A most violently idiosyncratic house . . .'

Built in Holt, Norfolk, Voewood was commissioned by the Reverend Percy Lloyd and his wife in 1900 – ten years after his father's death – and constructed between 1903 and 1905. It was built with the profits of the Lloyd family publishing fortune – they owned one of the most popular newspapers of the day and included so-called 'penny-dreadfuls' in their stable. An odd source of income for a vicar. Pevsner has described it as 'a most violently idiosyncratic house' and shortly after its completion, *Country Life* reviewed it and was of the opinion that, '. . . it does not fall into any defined architectural category'.[71] It is extraordinary, prepossessing, original and unique. Extraordinary in its adherence to the most extreme Arts and Crafts ideals in terms of honesty as it was built by direct labour and of materials from the ground that surrounds it. 'Mr Prior is a staunch protagonist in the demand that a building shall be racy of the soil it stands on', reported an apparently approving *Country Life* magazine.[72] Prepossessing in its unusual elevation and profile – 'an almost riotous variety of roof-line' – which still causes one to stop in one's tracks. Original in that it takes simple craft

techniques of decoration to a higher level than ever before. Put these factors together and you have a unique house. As the foundations were dug, the excavated stone and flint were sifted out to provide the decorative facings for the house, with the smallest pebbles added to the sand to make ballast for the concrete that forms the walls. Surplus materials were retained to form garden paths.

Built on a seven-acre former turnip field, the estate developed over several years, beginning with outbuildings including a pair of gardeners' lodges, heating shed, and stables – all possibly as a testing ground for Prior's unusual construction ideas before he turned his attention to the house. As his clerk of works, Prior employed Randall Wells, soon to be recognized as a significant architect in his own right and one who also worked for Lethaby at Brockhampton.

The main house is a further development of the butterfly plan used at Exmouth but with wings splayed at 60 degrees, compared to the more usual 45. These frame the enormous hall ('an obvious descendant of the feature beloved of our Saxon forebears'[73]) with its equally enormous inglenook fireplace, and open gallery. Largely symbolic, this fireplace is supplemented by an early central heating system concealed behind open wood panelling. One wing houses the service elements of kitchen, servants' sitting room, store rooms and kitchen giving onto the vegetable garden, whilst the other houses the library and billiard room. However, this wing is also the entrance façade with its entrance hall vaulted in reinforced concrete, and succeeds in masking the scale of Voewood and wrong-footing the visitor. At the entrance façade it presents itself as little more than a modest two-storey manor house with rather fanciful Tudoresque chimney stacks – one 'plain', one 'fancy', the two wedded together for effect. The butterfly plan, as at The Barn, is used to make the most effective layout of garden and terraces and by creating a suntrap with open loggias. Unlike Exmouth the scale of the building at Holt creates an interior of long vistas, odd angles and disorientations. Surely there is no better description of this remarkable house than that of the architect Roderick Gradidge who wrote that, 'It looks as though it is covered with a very old Fair Isle pullover that had been knitted by an imbecile child', and concluded, 'quaintness can be carried no further.'[74] Sadly the Reverend Lloyd only lived here for a few years as he sold up and moved to Italy following his wife's death.

Finally no assessment of Prior's career would be complete without looking at St Andrew's, Roker (1905–07), one of the handful of great Arts and Crafts churches that includes St Edward the Confessor, Kempley, by Randall Wells; Philip Webb's St Martin's, Brampton; and most of all Lethaby's All Saints', Brockhampton.

## St Andrew's, Roker

Built as a memorial to Jane Priestman, the mother of local shipbuilding millionaire John Priestman (who donated £6,000 for its construction), it is situated in a new suburb of expanding Sunderland. Further fundraising began in 1903 and Priestman was a demanding client, laying down strict conditions to secure his donation. These included his approval of the designs, that the church seat a congregation of 700, have uninterrupted views of the chancel and the inducement that – if completed by 31 December 1905 – he would pay the vicar's salary, on condition he chose him.

Like Prior's first church, Bothenbury, it is on an elevated and exposed position facing the sea. What faces the sea is the east end – this is no ordinary east end but an east end that seems to start with a tall, defiant tower. This is wrong. Towers are usually found at the west end of a church, or over a central crossing separating nave from chancel, the laity from the clergy, the sacred from the secular. A glance to the side of the

Textural quality again comes to the fore in the roughly fashioned stone walls of St Andrew's, Roker, pierced by the simple savagery of the tracery.

The east and west end windows at Roker are built up in sections almost like building blocks – a technique Ruskin would have approved of. Despite this almost primitive form of construction, they contain glass painting by Henry Payne of great beauty and delicacy with subjects drawn from everyday life.

north face of the tower reveals a stair turret redolent of Anglo-Saxon architecture with triangular headed windows. This suggestion is then reinforced by the triangular headed east and west end windows, equally savage, and equally Anglo-Saxon in their connotations. Prior, a devout Anglican who had no truck with the Oxford Movement, Pugin, or Anglo-Catholicism, was connecting with the history of the Early Christian Church all around in this windswept part of northern England. Just down the road is Monkwearmouth Priory, further afield Jarrow, Escomb, and Lindisfarne. This is the land of St Cuthbert, the Venerable Bede, and

The enormous transverse arches – first used at Bothenhampton – dominate the nave of St Andrew's.

the magnificent font designed and carved by Wells.

Wells contributed much more than the font. Styling himself 'resident architect', he acted as Prior's clerk of works but clearly contributed much more. Reviews published after completion of the church describe the building as by Prior and Wells, and in a letter to *The Builder* by Prior published in 1907 he wrote, 'I need scarcely add how much the appearance of the church has been due to his personal supervision, and in some cases actual handicraft upon the building', and claimed that the advanced construction '. . . is due entirely to him'.[75] The church was built by direct labour and thus not only maintained an important Arts and Crafts Movement ideal, but also saved costs for a church that had to be built quickly and to budget. Wells had also acted as Lethaby's clerk of works on All Saints', Brockhampton, completed several years earlier. But this experience wasn't as happy for Lethaby as it was for Prior.

Early Christianity. And it shows in Prior's manipulation of this Christian heritage.

Also, like Bothenbury, it is technically exhilarating with the interior created by an enormous series of five concrete transverse arches – on a scale that would swallow Bothenbury whole – creating an enormous undivided internal space for the congregation of 700. These arches are faced in the same roughly dressed, highly porous Marsden limestone that is used extensively throughout and supports reinforced concrete purlins. In turn these arches rest on double hexagonal columns, each surmounted by crude capitals that form the semblance of side galleries, or walkways. They are in fact also internal buttresses allowing the tall, shallow, and largely ineffective external buttresses which again speak of Anglo-Saxon architecture. These then surprise, as at Bothenbury, by projecting above the parapet to reveal their actual depth and strength.

The Marsden limestone used throughout the church is not amenable to fine carved detail and so gives an instantly aged, rough, weathered appearance. Internally the church is a showpiece of work by leading artist-craftsmen of the movement – furniture and fittings by Gimson and the Sapperton school, stained glass by Henry Payne (1868–1939), the reredos tapestry by Burne-Jones, Eric Gill (1882–1940) to carve the memorial tablet, his brother, Mac-Donald Gill (1884–1947), to paint the chancel, and

The font possesses an exceptionally primitive feeling – its hard, raw, porous Marsden limestone was carved by Randall Wells.

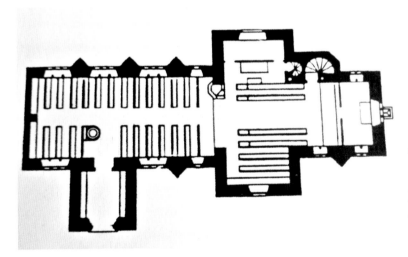

All Saints', Brockhampton. How old is it? It's almost impossible to date from its details unless you knew it was new in 1902.

Roker together with Lethaby's All Saints', Brockhampton stand out as the two great churches of the Arts and Crafts Movement. In so far as they have any precedents (and it's very hard to see that they do) it is surely Sedding's earlier Holy Trinity, Sloane Square. But Sedding's great work, completed by Lethaby's great friend Henry Wilson following Sedding's death in 1891, is still historicist albeit suave and sophisticated where they are rough and elemental, primitive in their associations, and innovatively daring in their construction.

Completed in 1902, Brockhampton was Lethaby's last building and the one that caused him most problems, possibly leading him to abandoning architecture as a profession after nearly two decades. Yet Nikolaus Pevsner called it '. . . one of the most convincing and most impressive churches of its date in any country'.[76] At first sight it's hard to see why. Outwardly it presents the timeless image of a typical English parish church from its rough sandstone walls, and wooden belfry, through to its immaculate thatch and quiet country setting. But this is far from being a traditional building for in designing it, as usual for the great theoretician of the Arts and Crafts Movement, Lethaby went back to first principles in so many ways, making it appear timeless. Peter Blundell-Jones put it well when he wrote that, 'A telling feature of Brockhampton is the difficulty of putting a precise date on it, even to the experienced eye.'[77] At every turn what is at first a familiar face – lancet windows, tracery, buttresses, a cruxiform plan – become strangers, something is always just slightly different, the correct historic detail just missing, or transmuted in some way. The lancets are more pointed than they should be, the 'medieval' tracery follows an unusual contorted pattern, the simple triangular buttresses are more like cut-waters on a stone bridge in their rawness, and the plan is devised to play tricks with the interior lighting.

In all probability the commission came Lethaby's way as a result of his days with Shaw when he

Roughly-dressed stone walling and crisply laid thatch at the east end. The triangular buttress almost suggests an anthropomorphic reading of this composition – an owl perhaps?

had worked on his master's All Saints' Church, Richards Castle, Shropshire, to which it has some similarities in its partly domestic character. Lethaby's client at Brockhampton, Alice Jordan, was the American wife of Arthur Foster, and commissioned the church from Lethaby as a memorial to her parents. Ten years earlier her aunt, Mrs Johnston Foster, had commissioned Shaw to design the church at Richards Castle so, as Godfrey Rubens speculates, she '. . . must, therefore have known Lethaby'.[78] Alice Foster lived in Brockhampton Court, the former rectory, which she and her mill-owning husband had rebuilt and where the original

semi-ruinous parish church was now in their grounds.

Lethaby was by this stage both Principle of the Central School of Arts and Crafts in London, and Professor of Ornament and Design at the Royal College of Art, so was hard pressed to have supervised construction. However, he was not one to put the construction out to tender, to risk losing control of the finished building and abandon this central tenet of Arts and Crafts ideology. Accordingly he appointed Wells as clerk of works – his eyes and ears on the job – and the church was built by direct labour. This might have been alright had this clerk not been a young

Two quatrefoil windows separated by a simple stone column admit a low light to the east end whilst accentuating the thickness of the wall. The ledge contains a shallow piscina for washing the holy vessels after their use. To the exterior its discreet presence is barely hinted at.

architect himself and keen on experimenting, and Lethaby, equally eager to continue exploring the possibilities of concrete roofs, had begun only the year before at the chapel of St Colm and St Margaret, for Melsetter House on Hoy.

Looking at the drawings for the church, the radical roof design went through three different iterations. The first drawings, dated 25 April 1901, show oak purlins running between transverse stone arches to form the roof. The second still shows wooden purlins but with coke-breeze concrete to the wall heads into which thatch is secured.

Finally, in a drawing of 28th May, it is poured concrete rather than oak purlins that spans each bay. This in turn is covered not with roofing tiles, as was intended in the original design, but thatch once again. Beyond the sheer experimental nature of the construction – perhaps exemplifying what Lethaby had termed 'the architecture of adventure' – it is hard to account for. Thatch, being lighter than tile and therefore reducing the weight pressing down on the untried concrete, may have been a simple rational decision. But why to have used concrete so daringly in the first place – thought of as a

thoroughly unartistic material – is harder to understand. In practical terms it worked well as the concrete absorbs the heat and releases it slowly during the day, whilst the thatch protects the concrete and keeps it cool; so it has been shown to be a thermally efficient way of building a church roof – and one largely without precedent.

So too is much of the decoration of the church. As we have seen in his first commission, Avon Tyrrell, Lethaby was fond of working with tradition whilst making it new. At Brockhampton this approach makes itself manifest from first sight. Whilst there is a traditional central crossing tower, this then competes, quite needlessly, with a wooden belfry erected over the porch. Once inside it is apparent that the central tower is not for hanging bells, but is merely a lantern to admit light into the centre of the church, separating the nave from the chancel. The same separation, of the sacred and secular, is signalled in the windows. To the nave they are smallish, squarish, and set thickly into the wall – so thick that each light has to be supported by internal stone columns. The modicum of light they admit creates a sense of mystery in the church despite their domestic character (to the chancel the windows are given the status of sanctity by the insertion of recognizable quatre-foil cusps). The mystery, or perhaps an attitude of primitive Christianity, that

Light floods in from the tower over the central crossing to reveal the transverse arches, which support an early concrete roof. The marks from the wooden shuttering are left for all to see.

leant against each other to form a primitive arch, without curves. It's almost Saxon in its directness and simplicity. It's the same shape of arch that greets the visitor at the porch. But this porch is also where the bells, situated in the wooden bell chamber above, would have to be rung, so the faithful on entering the church for a service might well be met by bell-ringers in a form of ritual arrival. The wooden belfry is a wonderful piece of vernacular building and rises out of the stone rim of the porch in a manner very reminiscent of the tower of All Saints', Richards Castle where the belfry in stone is set back from the tower and its porch, and contains a small run of mullioned windows not dissimilar to those in the nave wall at Brockhampton. Could it be that Lethaby had more of a hand in the design of Richards Castle

pervades the church is aided by the acutely pointed transverse arches that spring fully formed from low down in the nave walls, a vanishing trick already seen in Prior's church at Bothenbury.

The nave presents something of a cave-like, or up-turned boat, spectacle that immediately hushes the visitor on entry. The pointed arch is of course familiar, it's Gothic, and yet its point is too pointy, its angles too severe. Ruskin had argued – and Lethaby agreed – that a Gothic building could still be Gothic, savage, and rude if flat lintels were

Nikolaus Pevsner has called All Saints' '. . . perhaps the most thrilling church in any country of the years between historicism and the Modern Movement.' It's easy to see why in this picture.

A unique gargoyle design – as if the first there had ever been. Its primitivism is underscored by the carved vernacular pattern similar to that on the font at nearby Kempley, and again by the word PAX. Elsewhere the lead gutters are also decorated with the same early Christian suggestion.

built at the same time as Richards Castle – but in wood – the astonishing Byzantine Revival Church of the Holy Wisdom of God, Lower Kingswood (1891–92), designed by Sidney Barnsley. Lethaby's belfry is weather-boarded, with a prominent decorative wavy weather strip to each corner, its diagonally framed windows set high just beneath the pyramid roof, echoing the cross bracing of the construction hidden within.

As originally designed, the belfry was to have been the dominant tower but during the course of construction the decision was taken (it's been suggested by Wells without reference to either the client or the architect) to raise it by ten feet. This has the effect of the tower complementing, if not challenging, the belfry for dominance and it takes on an almost military, or fortified character appropriate to this border area. To its plain parapet is a crude pattern of chevrons in stone, again reminiscent of pre-Conquest Saxon architecture such as the tower of Earls Barton, the windows in Deerhurst, and the carvings to Clovelly in Lethaby's home county of Devon. But even though the belfry may have taken a few design cues from elsewhere, it remains a remarkably unique structure unlike anything else in English church, or domestic, architecture.

Against the heavy, fortified character of the structure and its attendant primitive and sparse

than acknowledged, or that the church had a greater influence on him than he admitted? It replaced a medieval church with a rare detached bell-tower of strikingly similar proportions to the central tower of Brockhampton and, as a pre-Conquest site with connections to Early Christianity, Richards Castle must have excited Lethaby's historical imagination. This unusual belfry also has echoes of another

A section of the east window with stained glass by Christopher Whall.

decoration to gutters, belfry, porch and parapet, the altogether exotic sinuous tracery leads to a more naturalistic scheme of decoration based on nature seen in the carved choir stalls. Although clear glass, in small windows, dominates the lighting of the interior, stained glass is placed in the east end window peopled with Pre-Raphaelitesque figures that mirror those in Burne-Jones' tapestries hung either side of the altar.

Lethaby's interest in Byzantine architecture clearly manifests itself in the running grapevine motif on the font immediately on the left as you enter. It can also be seen in the extraordinary pattern of window tracery to the tower, and

There is a Byzantine feel to the carving on the font reflecting Lethaby's growing interest in that style of art.

A strikingly original window to the tower. As at Avon Tyrrell, Lethaby takes familiar designs and reworks them to become something thrillingly new.

north transept. As readily seen as an adventure in Gothic – Blundell-Jones wrote that, 'This unGothic essay in Gothic tracery is a masterpiece' [79] – it again takes its cues from Byzantine architecture.

Wells was not the most conscientious of clerks of works and when an arch collapsed in the course of construction the worried client, Arthur Foster, wrote to Lethaby. Wells hadn't kept Lethaby informed. Then as it neared completion cracks began to appear in the south transept, indicating a problem in the foundations. Lethaby wrote to his wife Edith in despair and paid for all the remedial work himself and, so embarrassed by his poor supervision, refused to take his fee. Once finished, Wells moved a few miles away to design the remarkable church of St Edward the Confessor, Kempley. Lethaby never built again.

# Chapter 5

# When a Movement Becomes a Style

I<small>T IS A MOOT POINT WHETHER THE A<small>RTS AND</small></small> Crafts Movement would have developed as it did were it not for the generation of young architects that emerged from Norman Shaw's office. However, we shouldn't forget that the inspiration provided to this second generation of the Arts and Crafts Movement by figures such as Ruskin, Morris, Webb and Mackmurdo was available to all and continued to exert an influence to many others who followed them. Notable amongst this third generation were the architects Charles Voysey, M.H. Baillie Scott, and Sir Edwin Lutyens.

## Charles Voysey; '. . . the cottage is his ideal'

It is surely a strange coincidence that the two Arts and Crafts architects who most pursued individuality lived next door to each other. However, the individuality of Voysey was a million miles away from that of his neighbour, Prior. Voysey perfected an instantly recognizable style that has become a shorthand for the Arts and Crafts Movement, and yet pursued it determinedly in the name of individuality. Perplexingly it was often the same individuality everywhere he built. This is not necessarily an adverse criticism but it is to note an even greater departure from the Arts and Crafts ideal of only using local materials and building traditions than seen in Prior's increasing preference for texture over locality.

Opposite: An elegant window stay with a monkey-tail handle designed by Voysey. (© The Landmark Trust)

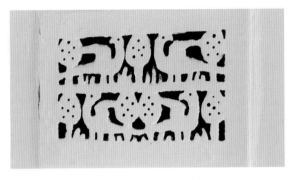

A simple ventilation block, the grille pierced by a bird, or two, in the bush. The attention Voysey gave to it perfectly illustrates his belief that nothing is too small or insignificant to be made beautiful. (© The Landmark Trust)

A page from the visitors' book of Voysey's Winsford Cottage Hospital in Devon shortly after it opened. It shows the cartoonist from *Punch* magazine in bed - he wrote underneath 'If I am to be ill, please may I be brought here'. (© The Landmark Trust)

Voysey's views on the matter were put forward in 1915 in his small book *Individuality*, where he sets out his credentials as the most uncompromising of artist-architects. It is very much an alignment of his religious views with his design principles as he claimed, 'I have written these chapters in the earnest hope of encouraging my fellow-men to believe and feel the creative spirit within everyone.'[80] Elsewhere in the book, despite a distaste for Morris, he nonetheless seems to restate the older man's famous dictum on beauty and utility by writing that, 'To the generous mind no detail is too small, or too insignificant to be worthy of our efforts to make it beautiful.' His work is a perfect testament to this belief.

John Betjeman remembered him as:

> . . . small, clean-shave and bird-like. He wore black suits and his coats had no cuffs or lapels to them, as he considered these non-functional survivals of eighteenth-century foppery. He wore saxe blue shirts and a blue tie in a gold ring. He smoked a clay pipe. Daily he walked up St James' to sit in the Arts Club and drink sherry and argue . . . He disliked Morris 'because he was an atheist.' . . . This account of Voysey may make him sound crotchety and cantankerous whereas in truth he was a generous, humorous and a fundamentally honest man.[81]

Maybe his fierce individuality – Lutyens observed of him that he '. . . was building – it was evident – what he liked'[82] – can be partly accounted for by being born and bred a Yorkshireman, and partly by aspects of that upbringing being by a father who was the vicar of Healaugh and sensationally expelled from the Church of England for his radical views. At the age of fourteen the young Charles and his family relocated to London where his father founded the Theistic Church. Charles was admitted to Dulwich School but failed to settle and so his formal education was completed under his father's influence. He was then articled, aged seventeen, to J.P. Seddon (1827–1906), a Goth and friend of Morris (for whose company he designed furniture). In 1880 he entered the office of George Devey – incidentally a member of his father's Theistic Church – for two years. Here he gained not only further experience in traditional design but also useful experience on a building site when Devey handed over a large job supervising the construction of cottages in Northamptonshire. This gave him just the kind of direct building experience

that was central to the Arts and Crafts ethos.

In 1931 *The Architectural Review* devoted a whole issue to Voysey's work. Whilst he acknowledged the importance of the Arts and Crafts Movement on him, he seems to have viewed it rather differently to others. There is little attention paid to the usual key figures such as Webb, and he barely mentions Morris. It seems like a deliberate oversight. Perhaps he shared his neighbour's view of Webb as actually a shrewd businessman – but then so was Voysey. For Voysey the significant figure was Mackmurdo, who had encouraged him to become a pattern-designer as well as an architect – a field he came to excel in.

Classicism was the enemy to Voysey and he despaired of the direction architecture was taking, recalling that, '. . . very soon after Shaw's time the Classicism of the Georgian type became fashionable and corrupted even the Great Lutyens.'[83] Those fellow architects of the Domestic Revival he might have been expected to admire – such as Guy Dawber – he dismissed as 'peasant-like.' Amongst his other influences were the illustrator Randolph Caldecott – an influence also acknowledged by Lutyens. That may go some way to explain his oversized details, large doors, pure forms, and the pursuit of a general simplicity akin to a doll's house.

More than many similar architects, Voysey managed to successfully bring the simple life of the country cottage idiom, writ large, into the town and put it at its ease in houses such as Annesley Lodge in Hampstead (1896). In other respects, he became the designer of a version of relaxed upper-middle class domestic architecture, which characterized the last century and suburban living generally. Spacious, simple, many-gabled, with rows of standard-sized metal casement window openings, roughcast, meticulous, with an absence of decorative detail, and set in just enough greenery to separate it from its neighbour, in his houses – beginning with his own at Chorley Wood, Hertfordshire of 1899 – Voysey perfected the large semi-detached house taken up so enthusiastically after the First World War. By 1926 he had designed almost 120 such private houses.

A picture of domesticity: Voysey's own house, The Orchard, Chorleywood. Is this the ideal for every suburban house since? Its front door differs only in detail and not intent from that for The Homestead.

## Early career

His professional career began in 1882 from a studio in Broadway Chambers, Westminster and where he entered into a short-lived partnership with his cousin Richard Voysey to become Voysey & Voysey. Amongst his early works was a (unexecuted) design for the South Devon Sanatorium Company in Teignmouth. This shows a very clear indebtedness to Shaw's Old English style with its Cragside-like profile of towers, battlements, and half-timbering, but with a patterned Tudoresque diapered brickwork more reminiscent of

The Homestead, Essex. The gables rise and fall to follow the land and the function of the rooms beneath. Note the carefully placed windows to the side of the chimney stack, indicating an inglenook. The clarity of Voysey's calligraphy is matched by his handling of materials generally. (Lawrence Weaver, *Small Country Houses of To-day*, 1922)

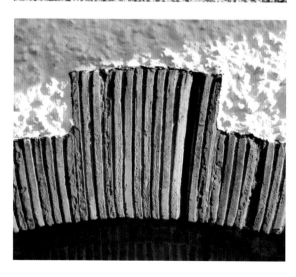

Devey. During these early years he joined both the Art Workers' Guild and exhibited at the first show of the Arts and Crafts Exhibition Society at the New Gallery, something he was to do in every subsequent exhibition. This would seem to imply a feeling for the crafts but is also evidence of his clubability – Voysey not only seeing the guild (which he became a Master of in 1924) as useful for networking but the exhibitions as an important means of publicity. Doubtless he was not alone in this. Much of this exhibited work was for wallpaper and textiles, which he used to supplement his income as an architect, whilst his distinctive furniture makes its first appearance in 1893. Yet he kept the two worlds quite separate and any examination of his preferred interiors show them largely devoid of his own decorative work save for metalwork and furniture. Wallpaper – as with most Arts and Crafts architects – had no place in his own home. So in a sense there are two Voyseys – the accomplished pattern-designer and guildsman encouraged by Mackmurdo (who he went on to design a house for in Hans Road, London in 1894) and Voysey the architect who evolved a stripped back pattern-language for his architecture of long, low buildings, covered in roughcast, with spare and simple decoration and everything gathered in under a large slate roof with wide projecting eaves.

## Honing the style

The style begins to emerge in 1885 in his unexecuted design for a house for himself and his wife. Long and low with the ground floor set back in such a way as to make the upper storey seem like a medieval guildhall or elongated Kentish Wealden house, nonetheless certain characteristics of the mature style are already present. Roughcast shares the restricted palette of materials with the timber close-studding which he gradually rejects as an unnecessary and expensive historicism. The long, low, horizontal nature of the house is emphasized and reinforced by the long, unbroken ridge line to the roof and also by the rows of simple rectangular casement windows.

Tall, elongated chimney stacks seem to be balanced by the equally etiolated and gently canted buttresses that disappear into the plane of the wall-surface at the last minute – the two elements appearing almost connected. And finally he makes a feature of the wide eaves that reinforce the image of safety and security and by giving status to the gutter supports – simple, meticulous, and elegantly detailed.

The house wasn't built but these themes are picked up in the first house he did complete at Bishop's Itchington, Warwickshire, in 1888, made perhaps less 'cottagey' by the removal of the half-timbering. As Muthesius commented, 'The cottage is his ideal, even when he is building houses of a size and luxuriousness more appropriate to a palace rather than a cottage.'[84] Other modest changes included breaking up the roof surface by the shallowest of dormer windows and the addition of a projecting porch, but in most other respects it's a realization of the unexecuted design. His next significant job, Walnut Tree Farm at Castlemorton of 1890, sees the rear roof pulled down the full length of the house in a daring catslide roof, made all the more dramatic by a roof pitch of 45 degrees, whilst to the front the dormers are more pronounced and given prominent half-timbered gables. The continuity developed between Bishop's Itchington and Walnut Tree Farm consolidates his basic vocabulary from this point.

Voysey's mature style begins to be clearly seen around 1890 at Walnut Tree Farm near Malvern – despite still clinging to some elements of historicism such as the half-timbered gable. (© Historic England)

He also introduces an element that becomes part of his artistic signature. This was the morning room, which stretches out behind an increasingly dominant series of tall projecting bay windows that light the double-height spaces. It's as if a medieval oriel window, used to light a great hall from the side, was now the focal point of the room and orientated to take advantage of the best views. These rooms become increasingly sophisticated in plan and elevation – with bays varying from being octagonal, or polygonal, to semi-circular and sometimes being taken not only to the full height of the wall but breaking through the eaves to form a dormer window or even a semi-submerged tower.

Yet Voysey's individuality was severely challenged (as was the Arts and Crafts Movement generally) by the increasing introduction of building control regulations and local bye-laws. These he, and others, saw as restricting his creativity, and therefore the search for his cherished individuality. The bye-laws and early building regulations were seen as further evidence of an inartistic mechanistic society and which, indirectly, held back progress in housing reform where building cheaply, but well, was seen as one of the ways to improve the lot of the working class. The movement's architects were, of course, caught between a rock and a hard place with this issue. Whilst they would be the last people to defend poor standards and jerry-building – one of the characters in *Beauty's*

*Awakening* was called 'Jerrybuiltus' – they struggled with the sort of regulations created to raise standards to the benefit of the least well off if it interfered with their freedom to design as unfettered artists. SPAB, stepping outside of their remit somewhat, opposed the local building regulations in Letchworth and won. And it was at Letchworth that the idea of 'the cheap cottage' that could bypass building regulations was first promoted on a national scale. Accordingly at Walnut Tree Farm, Voysey used a significant amount of half-timbering for the last time, not merely because of its historicism but because bye-laws no longer allowed it to be applied direct to the wall surface due to being a fire risk. Henceforth his exteriors become large expanses of white-painted roughcast broken only by the even, calm, pattern of his windows.

## Maturity: Perrycroft and Broadleys

### Perrycroft

Perrycroft (1893–94), situated in Colwall on the Malvern Hills, and not that far from Walnut Tree Farm, is where Voysey's various motifs and planning ideas come together to perfection for the first time. Built for the Birmingham industrialist and MP John William Wilson, it has magnificent views from its hillside vantage point near the ancient British camp

Perrycroft stares out from the Malvern Hills. The essentials of Voysey's style – long, low lines, tall inclined buttresses disappearing into the wall, wide eaves and even rows of casement windows – are captured here by the architectural illustrator Raffles Davison. (Raffles Davison, *Modern Homes*, 1909)

into Wales. This frontage has all the characteristics of Voysey – especially its gently sloping buttresses, which look like they are for decorative effect but are actually necessary for support. Voysey, in an attempt to keep costs down, built thin walls but with strong, tall buttresses, and then, by the generous application of roughcast, effectively added an extra layer of insulation for less cost than a thicker wall. As the journalist Horace Townsend reported in *The Studio* magazine, 'He considers a nine-inch brick wall faced with cement roughcast is as warm and weather-tight as any much more expensive construction.'[85] Perrycroft's proportions are long and low and sheltered under one simple slate roof with wide projecting eaves. Voysey liked his buildings to have repose and relax into their sites and, as with so much of his work, he wrote interestingly on the subject in *Individuality*, arguing that, '. . . when we are weary we recline, and the darkness covers up the differences and hides all detail under one harmonious veil, while we too, close our eyes for rest.' What was necessary in good house design for Voysey was '. . . to avoid angularity and complexity in colour, form or texture, and make our dominating lines horizontal rather than vertical.' This repose is found in the typical Voysey interior where ceilings are kept low – creating the cottage feel – materials left to speak for themselves – following Ruskin – or painted white to complement the exteriors. Colour was found in simple, modest tilework to his elegant fire surrounds. Staircases in particular seemed to fascinate him, as did entrance halls, and effectively became small buildings in their own right, whilst corridors are kept narrow, with doors made '. . . wide in proportion to height, to suggest welcome – not stand-offishly dignified, like the coffin lid, high and narrow for the entrance of one body only.'[86]

## Broadleys

Perrycroft set the standards by which Voysey's work over the next twenty years work can be judged – seen in buildings such as The Homestead, Moor Crag, The Orchard, and Hill Close, Studland. But if Perrycroft is

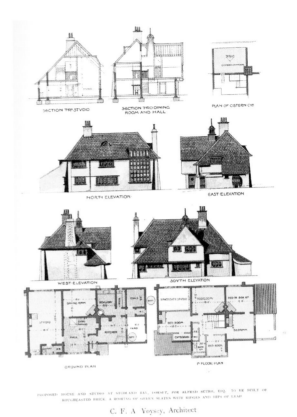

Drawings for a studio house at Studland Bay, Dorset. Notice the full height window to light the studio. (W. Shaw Sparrow, *The Modern Home*, 1906)

Voysey's most representative building then Broadleys, one of his few grander houses, is surely his finest. As Wendy Hitchmough has written, 'There was no single artistic focus to Broadleys. The brilliance of the design unfolded in a sequence of subtle and sometimes surprising revelations.'[87] Magnificently sited above Lake Windermere, it has the same complexity of plan as Perrycroft but not the ambiguity over the entrance or idiosyncrasies of decoration. The steepness of the site allowed Voysey to add a lower ground floor to the north service wing, and the views of the house from the lake are dominated by the three full-height bowed windows which break through the eaves into the equally steep roof of beautifully graduated Westmoreland slate.

In his houses in the Lake District he was at least using local materials appropriate to the local area and

Broadleys is often seen as Voysey's finest house, its three curvaceous bay windows affording spectacular views over Lake Windermere and to the fells beyond. (Above: Creative Commons Attribution-Share Alike 3.0 Unported)

at Broadleys seems to have overseen the construction himself with regular visits taking place. At the same time as Broadleys was being constructed, he was also building Moor Crag, only a quarter of a mile away, and so could easily combine site visits (whilst charging his

clients twice for expenses!). Initially orientated to the south-east to maximize daylight, Voysey broke this strong preference to take full advantage of the magnificent view. Moor Crag was constructed in 1898–1900 as a holiday home for the Wakefield colliery owner Arthur Currer Briggs; Muthesius gave it extensive coverage and Voysey exhibited it at both the Arts and Crafts Exhibition Society and the Royal Academy. After commissioning Voysey to design this holiday home, the client went on to commission buildings for his workforce at Whitwood in 1905, including a terrace of twenty-nine houses, a manager's house, and a Miners' Institute.

Writing in *The Studio* in 1907, Baillie Scott tried '. . . to sum up in a few words the scope and purposes of Mr Voysey's work, one might say that it consists mainly in the application of serenely sane, practical and rational ideas to home making.'[88]

## M.H. Baillie Scott: – '. . . the artistic house'

The same might be said of Mackay Hugh Baillie Scott – a great admirer of Voysey – and where we reach one of the peaks of Arts and Crafts architecture for its consistently captivating qualities. He is an architect who Muthesius celebrated as one of 'the purely northern poets among British architects.' Born in Broadstairs, Kent, the eldest of fourteen children, he originally trained in agriculture at the national Agricultural College in Cirencester, his Scottish father being a major landowner whose wealth came from extensive sheep-farms in Australia. These, his eldest son seemed destined to manage at this stage and they provided him with a modest private income for much of his life. With the Agricultural College situated in the very heart of the Cotswold group of craftsmen centred on Gimson and the Barnsleys at Sapperton, it is hard not to believe that this wasn't an influence but there is no evidence of any contact between the young man and the Sapperton group. In 1886, shortly after completing his course, he became articled to the City Architect of Bath, Major Charles Davis (1827–1902). To have been trained in the office of an official architect, a category castigated by those in private practice for their lack of individuality and originality, is an interesting start to one of the most successful professional careers of any Arts and Crafts architect, especially for one who became so noted for his individuality and artistry.

Whatever else he may have benefitted from in Bath, it was there that he also met his future wife. In 1889 the newlyweds moved to the Isle of Man, where Baillie Scott quickly entered into partnership with Frederick Saunderson, a surveyor and land agent, whom he met whilst studying at the local art college in Douglas. The Isle of Man may seem an odd choice despite having a somewhat captive local clientele. An architectural journalist who knew him in the 1930s recalled, '. . . in his sleepy, laconic way with his melancholy expression, half-shut eyes and drooping moustache, Baillie Scott would simply say what happened, "I went to the Isle of Man for a holiday. I was so seasick I couldn't face the journey back so I set up in practice there".'[89]

### The Manxman

Certainly this Manx episode, lasting from 1889 to 1901, is possibly the most productive period of Baillie Scott's working life. Its strong ancient Viking culture became a notable influence on his work as did the teachers in the Douglas School of Art where he not only studied himself, but later taught. Amongst his more notable colleagues was Archibald Knox (1864–1933), one of the most accomplished silversmiths and decorative artists of his day. His work sold from Liberty's department store in London, and delighted in Celtic motifs drawn from the island's history. In the true collaborative spirit of the Arts and Crafts Movement, Baillie Scott and Knox worked together on several commissions for decorative work, Baillie Scott thereby earning himself a considerable reputation as that Arts and Crafts ideal of the all-round

designer. These early works on the Isle of Man included several houses (such as Oakleigh, Holly Bank, Ivydene, Laurel Bank, and his own, the Red House) and in Onchan the village hall, police station, and the Mansion. Many of these early Manx buildings show an indebtedness to Norman Shaw, Ernest George, and the architects of the Domestic Revival generally in their use of half-timbering, tile hanging, and asymmetrical picturesque profiles but soon he adopts Voysey's favoured white-painted roughcast, and much else, for his elevations and freely admits to much of his early work being influenced by the older man. As Betjeman noted, 'They both liked sloping buttresses, pebble-dash and picturesque chimneys. They both had their work illustrated in *The Studio*.'[90]

Island life did not isolate Baillie Scott as might be thought. In 1896, for example, he exhibited furniture, metalwork, and wallpaper designs at the Arts and Crafts Exhibition Society. Neither was he restricted to the island for his clients, taking the opportunity to exhibit some of his major works, such as Blackwell in the Lake District and the White House, Helensburgh, at the Royal Academy in 1899 and 1900 respectively. Additionally, he began to develop his career through the pages of *The Studio* with articles such as, 'The Decoration of the Suburban House' in 1895, and 'The Small Country House' in 1897 and where he began his assault on the typical poorly designed nineteenth-century terrace. Neither was his fame restricted to Britain. Such a profile in one of the leading artistic magazines of its day led to a commission in 1897 from Ernest Ludwig, the Grand Duke of Hesse, to decorate rooms in his ducal palace in Darmstadt. These were executed by Ashbee's Guild of Handicraft, the palace being set amidst an artists' colony the Duke was establishing.

### A growing reputation

Eventually in 1901 he left the island and settled in Bedford where he was close to J.P. White's joinery, the Pyghtle Works, which had been producing his

*HOUSE IN MEADWAY, HAMPSTEAD GARDEN SUBURB*
*M. H. BAILLIE SCOTT, Architect*

Baillie Scott's design for Meadway in Hampstead Garden Suburb shows how to cleverly carry a building around the sharp corner of a road junction. (Baillie Scott et al., *Garden Suburbs, Town Planning and Modern Architecture*, 1910)

Corrie Wood and Elmwood, two of the open-plan houses designed by Baillie Scott for Letchworth Garden City's 'Cheap Cottage' exhibition of 1905. One of the catslide roofs almost touches the ground. Elmwood is semi-detached but designed so it can easily be turned into a detached house; Baillie Scott deliberately flouted the rules of the competition. (Above: Corrie Wood courtesy of Charter Whyman)

furniture designs since 1898 and had just produced a catalogue promoting these. Bedford could also boast of fellow Arts and Crafts architects F.L. Griggs and C.E. Mallows (who also designed furniture for White) – both architects who shared Baillie Scott's artistic abilities. The planning and combination of rooms – be they for a house or flat – exercised him greatly as an architect and projects such as Falcon Cliff Terrace, Douglas, Meadway and Waterlow Court (his favourite building) in Hampstead Garden Suburb show him trying out various ideas to deal with mass-housing later developed more famously by Parker and Unwin.

Baillie Scott was increasingly favoured by publications such as *The Studio*, *The Studio Yearbook of Decorative Art*, in German publications such as *Dekorative Kunst* and in America's *House Beautiful*. In 1906, during a slack period of work in Bedford, he published his own book, *Houses and Gardens*, which was effectively his design manifesto for what was known as 'the artistic house'. In it he wrote of 'the artistic house' as not being based on:

> . . . frillings and ornaments, but on the very essence of its structure. The claims of common sense are paramount in its plan... No dusty carpets cover its floors. Its apartments are not crowded with useless and unlovely furniture. It aims at fulfilling no popular conception of what a house should be, follows no fashion.[91]

Often his beguiling watercolours – collected at the end of the book – were never realized but nonetheless had an impact on the advanced artistic tastes of the day. Those that were built included Blackwell, The White House, Bill House, several houses in Cambridge, and houses that contributed to the early development of the Garden City Movement. In Letchworth Garden City he designed Elmwood, Springwood, Tanglewood, and Corrie Wood, and shows his mature Arts and Crafts style at is best, combining good internal planning, sparse vernacular exteriors with sweeping catslide roofs, often enclosing a tour

An illustration of a 'cheap cottage' by Baillie Scott from the pages of *The Studio* (1914) demonstrates the idea of open-plan living by eliminating the parlour.

COTTAGE AT MILFORD, SURREY

M. H. BAILLIE SCOTT, ARCHITECT

de force of interior decorative effects in wood, metal, glass, plaster and textiles that few others equalled and relied on good proportions, sound construction and practical planning. Elmwood Cottages were designed for the 'Cheap Cottage Exhibition' but fell foul of the regulations, which stated they should be able to be built for £150 per unit – Elmwood (a pair of semi-detached cottages) cost £200 per unit.[92]

In particular Baillie Scott developed a form of small suburban house all but taken for granted today that he began in the 1890s and which comes to fruition in the years leading up to the First World War. In *Houses and Gardens*, he wrote of it as 'a roomy and commodious cottage, not a mansion in miniature'. It proved compelling as the years after its publication were his most productive. In Cambridge he designed no less than twelve new houses mainly for academics and their families in this idiom. A central concept was the hall house, that is to say a large central living space – perhaps capable of being sub-divided by sliding screens – off which everything else fed and which eliminated the need for wasteful corridor space. Privacy was sometimes provided by little more than an elaborate inglenook, a dining recess, or bay window that could open onto the garden. In other words, the open-plan house where Baillie Scott could manipulate (and decorate) the various elements depending on the size of the house, the budget,

This detail of a section of wall at Blackwell shows Baillie Scott's love of materials.

and the client. The handling of materials was no less important to him. Whilst wood panelling was to be planed smooth, most materials were not to be so highly finished. Structural timber, he argued, should retain its 'tree-ness' and the marks of the worker's adze. Plaster should be finished with a trowel, not a float, to retain the marks of its making and contain sharp sand to give a rough surface texture. Yet he did not pursue texture with the same zeal as Prior, writing that, 'There is no special merit in making any surface rough or smooth. Texture is mainly valuable in so far as it expresses the inherent character of the particular texture.' His hatred of the standard red-brick terrace of houses (he suggested they should all be called 'The Crimes') made him a natural acolyte of the Garden City Movement and so it is at Letchworth, Hampstead Garden Suburb and Gidea Park that his artistic ideas on housing came to the fore.

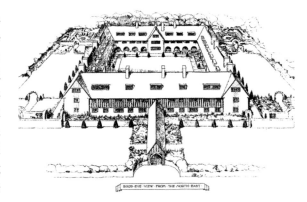

An enticing bird's-eye view drawing by Baillie Scott of the carefully cloistered life at Waterlow Court in Hampstead Garden Suburb. (Baillie Scott et al., *Garden Suburbs, Town Planning and Modern Architecture*, 1910)

## Waterlow Court

In Waterlow Court in Hampstead Garden Suburb (designed in 1904, built 1908–09), for housing reformer, Liberal MP and philanthropist Sir Sydney Waterlow (1822–1906), he designed an unusual monument to the early days of female emancipation in the shape of a block of fifty flats for single working women. Sir Sydney was well known to Henrietta Barnett, one of the prime movers behind the new suburb, and he had established the Improved Industrial Dwellings Company in the 1860s.

Waterlow is designed as a courtyard, or quad, with an internal arcaded walkway of broad semi-circular arches – so effectively an open cloister with hints of The Orchard, an early country house by Lutyens. Baillie Scott wrote that, 'In seeking for the type of plan which would be most suitable for such a group of houses, the College Court with its central hall and cloisters at once suggests itself.' It is approached through a long projecting timber-framed tunnel with brick noggin. Its grid-like portcullis gives it a certain military character, transforming it into more of a

Waterlow Court's portcullis-like entrance gates.

gateway or barbican than simple covered walkway. This martial note is quickly deflated by a relatively new building type – the ladies' bicycle shed.

The flats were designed for women of progressive political views who couldn't afford a servant, yet wished for company whilst retaining a degree of privacy. It may well be that the long timber walkway is a means of sparing the modesty of the inhabitants as they mounted and de-mounted their bikes. The accommodation is arranged over three floors (including the dormer-clad roof) of three- to five-roomed flats (each still based on the hall house concept with recesses – such as box beds – coming off) connected by regularly spaced stairs contrived in a vaguely Jacobean style, whilst meals were taken together in a communal dining hall. In *Houses and Gardens*, Baillie Scott argued that flats such as Waterlow Court should be designed as a country house, with the individual units stacked one on top of the other. Other communal facilities included a shared common room and kitchen, accommodation for the housekeeper, shared servants, and allotments. Simple plank doors characterize the building with Heal's supplying the doors and window furniture made by J.P. White of Bedford. Externally Baillie Scott has maintained the timber frame of the entrance to the upper floor set into walls of dark-purple stock bricks with a clay-tile roof and dressings, with decorative glazed tile work to the gables whilst internally the elevations are much plainer, being of simple whitewashed brick which immediately lifts the defensive air to one altogether lighter and more relaxed.

Such purpose-designed flats for women were far from common but are a notable feature of the Arts and Crafts Movement as it developed alongside the fight for women's rights. Other such buildings included hostels such as Ames House (1904), for the YWCA in Camden designed by Beresford Pite, and the Time and Talents Settlement building in Bermondsey, of 1908, by fellow guildsman Sir Reginald Blomfield.

## Edwin Lutyens – 'He took Shaw's place, but who is to take his?'

Waterlow Court (1908–09) has interesting parallels with Goddards (1898–1900) by Sir Edwin Lutyens, designed for Frederick Mirrielees. At first sight it resembles one of his typical Surrey houses of the period. But reviewing it in a 1904 *Country Life* magazine revealed it to be a holiday home intended for (amongst others) 'nurses from hospitals, ladies of small means who could not otherwise afford a holiday, East End workers exhausted by care for others' and who for two or three weeks had 'a bright social life there, readings, games and, perhaps best of all, a lovely garden.'[93] Only planned for six guests, and a custodian, Lutyens visited and wrote approvingly to his wife, 'Went down to Goddards and went over the

Lutyens uses broad areas of white-painted roughcast to dress, and undress, the fabric of Goddards. (© The Landmark Trust)

Not every house has its own skittle alley... but this was no ordinary house when first built. Note how a section of the bowl return can be lifted out to allow the outside door to function! (© The Landmark Trust)

place. It seems very successful and the inmates love it and invariably weep when they leave it, which is comforting. Mirrielees seems very happy with it too. . . . We all played a game of skittles in my alley! I like using the things I make.'[94]

Goddards only operated 'as a Home of Rest to which ladies of small means might repair for holiday' for the first ten years of its existence. In 1910 Mirrielees recommissioned Lutyens to extend the building to become a private house for his son Donald, and his new American wife, whilst the female guests were relocated to a converted nearby barn.

Composed of two-storey equal-length wings of bedrooms radiating off from the single-storey communal hall (with a games room above in the attic), the plan allowed the creation of a courtyard garden. As was normal for Lutyens, especially in Surrey, the gardens were laid out in collaboration with his friend, the garden designer Gertrude Jeykll (who had already worked for Mirrielees at his own house, Pasture Wood), most probably the person who introduced architect and client.

The conversion for the newlyweds entailed Lutyens extending both wings to create a large dining room in the north wing and a library in the south. Two additional bedrooms (less spartan than the originals) were added above with their own dressing rooms, and of course there was now a need for a bigger service

A carefully chamfered ledged and braced door opens onto the communal dining room and reveals the traditional wooden-framed construction that is hidden by the brickwork externally.
(© The Landmark Trust)

wing. Accordingly, three servants' bedrooms and a bathroom were fitted into the gallery and a further bedroom into the north wing. To make life easier central heating and electricity was now also incorporated, but on completion the newlyweds only spent weekends at Goddards.

Despite its interest as a piece of social history, architectural judgements have not been kind to it. A.S.G. Butler writing in 1950 claimed that:

Goddards shows Sir Edwin's skill in the conjunction of roughcast, moulded brick and Horsham stone slates . . . Yet there is a danger in the strong sympathy for material. It is too easy to over-exhibit it... For roughcast, moulded brick, stone and Horsham slates and ordinary roofing tiles are too rich an agglomeration in so small an area. It suggests a little that the architect wanted to display his great knowledge of all of them.[95]

## The Lutyens style

Lutyens (he was knighted in 1918) is often championed as the greatest English architect since Christopher Wren, perhaps greater. For some this great claim is built upon his early work as an architect of the Arts and Crafts Movement. For others it rests upon his turn to Classicism – so disapproved of by Voysey – from around 1906 signalled by the completion of Heathcote, a Classical villa in Ilkley. Betjeman recalls of his time working on *The Architectural Review* that, 'The only classical architect we were allowed to admire was Sir Edwin Lutyens. This was because he had in his youth been associated with the Arts and Crafts Movement . . . And anyhow Lutyens was a rebel. Hadn't he been in a row with the RIBA?'[96] A third claim to architectural immortality is his work at New Delhi in India – often seen as the great palace he never got the chance to build in England.

Given this stylistic liberalism, not to say betrayal, it is perhaps questionable if Lutyens should be included in a book on Arts and Crafts architecture at all. Nonetheless he has good credentials, having been trained in the office of Ernest George (where he would have worked with Guy Dawber, and where Herbert Baker was chief assistant) although he'd hoped to be articled to Shaw. He was also a member of the Art Workers' Guild (becoming its Master in 1933), opposed the idea of architects' registration (although as much because he didn't want the distinction between architect and surveyor to be so clear), advised would-be architects to spend time in a builder's yard as he had done as a child in rural Surrey, and valued traditional materials and craftsmanship over mass-production. Despite

Heathcote marked a radical stylistic departure for Lutyens – from Arts and Crafts to Classical. Voysey saw it as a betrayal.

these credentials Sir Robert Lorimer, often called 'the Lutyens of Scotland', remarked that '. . . I've always heard him derided by the Schultz school as a "Society" architect.'[97]

It is easy to understand why the 'Schultz school' – the Arts and Crafts Movement – formed this view. Lutyens moved in court circles due to family connections, flirted with the Royal Academy (being made an Associate in 1913, and a full Academician in 1920) and in so assiduously '. . . ministering to the swinish luxury of the rich' seems every inch the society architect. So at the very least, he is difficult to place. The conventional response to this would be that geniuses often are. In determinedly pursuing wealthy clients, he certainly seems an odd bed-fellow for Morris and Webb. Yet, like Lethaby, his admiration for Webb was unbounded. Writing of him later in life he confessed that, 'The freshness and originality which Webb maintained in all his work I, in my ignorance, attributed to youth. I did not recognize the eternal youth of genius though it was conjoined to another attribute of genius – thoroughness.'[98]

However there were compelling financial reasons for his pursuit of wealth in the shape of Lady Emily Bulwer-Lytton, his future wife, whose parents expected Lutyens to make an income commensurate with her status, and for much of his working life he was financially shackled to a life insurance policy of £11,000. This financial burden was clearly a strain on Lutyens and he admired his friends, such as his first client, Arthur Chapman (nicknamed 'Chippy') who had made his fortune establishing an import business in India. 'I can't help being jealous of Chippy,' he wrote to his wife, 'who has no living to make and all the spare time!'[99] Lutyens' houses smelt of money and the architect Harry Goodhart-Rendel (1887–1959) recollected the impression of being brought up in one where 'Everything was unexpected, fantastic . . .' but '. . . of course enormously expensive, which merely added a welcome cachet to ownership of "a Lutyens house".'[100] Due to these financial pressures he had an unwritten rule of refusing to meet with clients who had a budget of less than £20,000 and famously claimed of his wealthy client at Heathcote, textile millionaire James Hemingway, that he '. . . could not spend money until he met me.'[101]

## 'Small Country Houses of To-day'

As Gavin Stamp has commented, 'If not strictly suburban, most Lutyens houses are certainly not truly rural.'[102] One of the benefits of his wealthy clients was that they didn't need to play country cottages as they wanted large houses – and that is what Lutyens gave them, but not so large as to be the flagship for an estate supported by thousands of acres of agricultural land. Most of Lutyens' country houses were still essentially large villas set in a modest few acres to be used as holiday homes and aimed to fit into the local vernacular, like so many Arts and Crafts houses. The clients were usually the nouveau riche, not the established landed aristocracy. Nonetheless he also supplied the range of ancillary buildings, such as cottages, stables and lodges, which was a bonus and to these buildings he devoted almost as much care and attention as to the main house. It was here that the simpler Arts and Crafts building could be found defining the edges of a modest estate beneath the grandeur of the main house. In this respect he still reflects Ashbee's assertion that the Arts and Crafts Movement belongs in the countryside – a countryside he recreates for his clients in many ways. It is very noticeable that his Lutyens country houses tend to be vernacular, sometimes erring towards a Tudoresque revivalism; once he 'goes to town' his architectural response to an urban context is usually Classical, and more often Neo-Georgian; 'the architecture of good manners' as Trystan Edwards called it.

## Early Years

Lutyens established his own practice in 1888 when still quite young, with a modest half-timbered and tile-hung house, Crooksbury near Farnham, which

Munstead Wood brought Lutyens and the garden designer Gertrude Jekyll together for the first of a much-celebrated series of collaborations.

reflected the local Surrey vernacular but could also as readily have come off the drawing board of his master, Ernest George, or even Norman Shaw. 'It was great fun that first house,' he recalled later, 'I advise everyone to build a house at nineteen. It's such good practice . . . and I've been building them ever since.'[103] Lutyens went on to design further extensions to Crooksbury over the next twenty years. Muthesius spotted his talent early on and wrote of him that, 'He is a young man who has come increasingly to the forefront of domestic architects and who may soon become the accepted leader among English builders of houses.'

Not only did this commission also lead to Lutyens designing the local Liberal Club in Farnham (an early essay in crude Neo-Georgian) where the client was active in local politics, but it drew him to the attention of one of his two most important clients and future collaborators, the garden designer Gertrude Jekyll. In 1896 she commissioned him to design her own house, Munstead Wood, although initially it was merely for a modest house called The Hut in the grounds of the future house from where she laid out the garden. Elsewhere on the estate he designed a gazebo, a potting shed, a delightfully picturesque gardener's cottage and a stable block all held together by Jekyll's advanced ideas on garden design. This was

soon to become a working relationship that benefitted both individuals considerably and brought into being one of the most creative symbiosis between architect and gardener perhaps ever seen. Together Jekyll and Lutyens recreated the relationship between a house and its garden, and then the garden and its landscape setting. Equally influential was Lutyens' championing by *Country Life* magazine and its proprietor Edward Hudson – Lutyens' second most significant client after Jekyll.

## Munstead Wood

Munstead Wood began with the two friends touring the local area studying its vernacular architecture and plundering it for ideas for the new house. Its garden front is dominated by two large Webbian gables book-ended by two elongated Tudoresque chimney stacks of so prodigious a height they might have been by Shaw at his most excessive. Jekyll was to consolidate her interest in vernacular architecture in her book *Old West Surrey* (1904) although Ralph Nevill's earlier *Old Cottages and Domestic Architecture in South-West Surrey* of 1891 is usually seen as more influential. Leaded casement windows puncture the façade in even rows in the manner of Voysey,

Concave and complex. Lutyens' signature tall chimney stacks dominate this view of Tigbourne Court. A mixture of vernacular and early Renaissance influences inform the design – the rich texture to the wall surface being heightened by bands of terracotta tiles and gallets, with tiny pieces of dark stone placed into the mortar joints. (© Stefan Czapski and licensed for reuse under this Creative Commons Licence. geograph-3748297)

and the whole elevation is gathered in under a large simple roof of local hand-made clay tiles. This main elevation fronts the book room, and dining room, separated by a large hall that runs from the front to the back of the house to connect the garden terrace with the garden court. Constructed of local brown Bargate stone and constructional oak, it is laid out on a u-shaped plan enabling the creation of the garden court, which is overlooked by an overhanging timber-framed gallery or pentice, with curved members of the frame exposed for decorative effect, not unlike some of Baillie Scott's work.

Jekyll invited Hudson to visit. He was clearly impressed and it soon appeared in *Country Life*. Once complete Lutyens used The Hut at Munstead Wood from which to design his second major house, Orchards, in nearby Busbridge. This he received as a result of the work at Munstead Wood. The owner, glass manufacturer William Chance, had almost decided not to build on his recently bought site, having been disappointed by a design by Halsey Ricardo which he and his wife rejected. But then they saw Munstead Wood nearing completion and sought out the designer, the young Lutyens.

Munstead Wood was the first of a succession of country houses in a vernacular Arts and Crafts idiom (but gradually giving way to what Robert

Venturi and Denise Scott-Brown have termed 'the Anglicanization of Classicism') that included important country houses such as Sullingstead, Fulbrook House, Tigbourne Court, Orchards, Goddards, Deanery Garden and Folly Farm, Berrydown Court, Homewood, Marsh Court, Little Thakeham ('the best of the bunch', according to Lutyens), Papillon Hall, Grey Walls, Overstrand Hall, and even one in France, Le Bois des Moutiers – all developing the Munstead manner of a romantic vernacular country house. Lutyens' output was prodigious. Five of these commissions were all being built in the same year, 1897, at a time when he had twenty-five jobs. In 1906 he wrote to his wife that he had signed contracts for several buildings worth a total of £34,000 in one week. As he worked on a commission of five per cent of building costs, it must have been a very good week indeed.

## Deanery Garden

Of all these houses, it is Deanery Garden that is the most impressive. Designed for Edward Hudson, it was used by him in the pages of *Country Life* to be a showpiece for the young architect. Built in an old orchard and confined by an ancient brick wall held

Lutyens' Deanery Gardens as photographed for *Country Life* magazine. The full height oriel window floods the interior with light and balances the chimney stacks in the composition.

up by enormous buttresses, it is dominated by a marvellous double-height oriel window that lights the interior, outdoing Voysey in its grandeur. It is a tour de force of the bricklayer's skill, which is then balanced on the garden front by one of Lutyens' towering Tudoresque chimney stacks whose triangular profile is carried down into a canted full-height chimney breast of plain, unrelieved brickwork. The forty-eight individual frames of the giant oriel window seem to break out on this façade and run beneath the eaves of the over-sailing roof to extend the effect. The strong angular geometry and sense of proportion here contrast with the softer semi-circular reveals of the almost Romanesque doorway, which is then picked up in the garden – mirrored in the steps to the terrace and its enclosing walls. As Gavin Stamp has commented, 'Deanery Garden may be regarded as the quintessential Lutyens house.'[104] Tellingly the article on it in *Country Life* of 9 May 1903, in the section entitled 'Houses for people with hobbies', failed to mention that the 'people' in question was the

magazine's proprietor, Edward Hudson. Hudson sold the house only a few years after completion, adding to the speculation that Lutyens was being used as a vehicle to promote the magazine. Whatever the truth Hudson continued to befriend Lutyens and commissioned him to design not only the new offices for *Country Life* in Covent Garden in 1904 but two further residences – the conversion of Lindisfarne Castle to be another holiday home for him, and finally Plumpton Place.

By 1913 and the publication of Lawrence Weaver's *Houses and Gardens by E.L. Lutyens* by *Country Life*'s book publishing arm, one of Lutyens' assistants recalled, '. . . the whole of the aristocratic London world was at his feet. Clients continually came to the door, and the Aston Webb people were jealous – they were next door – when we had three more carriages than they had or when we had two noblemen and they had only one.' On his death one obituary elegiacally said, 'He took Shaw's place, but who is to take his?'[105]

Built with the proceeds of the brewing industry, Blackwell is one of a series of holiday homes designed by Arts and Crafts architects. (© Lakeland Arts, Right: Baillie Scott, *Houses and Gardens*, 1906)

GROUND FLOOR PLAN

FIRST FLOOR PLAN

Blackwell, at Bowness-on-Windermere, was built between 1898 and 1901, the original design being exhibited at the Royal Academy in 1898. It is one of the few houses of the Arts and Crafts Movement which has received almost universal acclaim, Muthesius calling it, '. . . a handsome house in beautiful surroundings on Lake Windermere. The house combines dignity with great comfort and a poetical atmosphere within.' And so it does. Muthesius' appreciation of the architect Baillie Scott may well have launched his considerable continental career. At the time of its completion Baillie Scott was thirty-six years old and a well-established architect, thanks to his promotion in the pages of *The Studio* magazine. His 1906 account of his own work and ideas, *Houses and Gardens*, included Blackwell amongst the projects he illustrated. Whilst it was the arrival of the railway which made this kind of development possible it is ironic that, notwithstanding the beauty of the building, this is probably just the kind of development that Ruskin, a resident of nearby Brantwood near Coniston, deplored for spoiling the beauty of the Lake District.

Despite having established his reputation by now, Blackwell was a significant commission for Baillie Scott due to its size. Originally the job was to have gone to Barry Parker and Raymond Unwin. Indeed Parker & Unwin's design reappeared as a speculative design for a '£10,000 house' in the pages of the *Daily Mail*. Under its proprietor, Lord Northcliffe, the newspaper was a promoter of housing reform, creating The *Ideal Home* Exhibition in 1908 to further its aims.

The house was designed as a holiday home for the Manchester brewer Sir Edward Holt (1849–1928) and his family of five children. In 1907 Edward became Lord Mayor of Manchester and amongst his many public works was helping improve the city's

What price for individuality? Here at Moor Crag in the Lake District the style remains the same as in Essex, Dorset, Hertfordshire or Worcestershire – it says simply 'vernacular'.

water supply by the creation of a reservoir in the Lake District. That his wealth came from brewing (Holt's Brewery is still going today) possibly made a good supply of clean water to Manchester even more desirable. It was this brewing wealth that allowed him to buy part of the former Storrs Hall estate in Bowness, which was auctioned off for development in 1889. Such wealth allowed the employment of a cook, four maids, two gardeners and a chauffeur to maintain the house for the family whilst on their holidays. Two other notable Arts and Crafts houses – Broadleys and Moor Crag, both by Voysey – were also built on the former Storrs Hall estate.

The house reaches for the sky high up above Lake Windermere with its principal rooms – drawing room, double-height hall with

recessed billiard room, dining room (all with typically Arts and Crafts inglenook fireplaces) and servants' hall facing south over manicured lawns to catch the best sunlight – the overall plan is an L-shape. To the north, the gabled entrance front is enclosed by an east-facing service wing, which creates a forecourt. From here the house is entered through a modest stepped entrance hall and cloakroom. These north and south ranges are separated by a simple straight corridor, or cross-passage – 'broad and low' wrote the architect – that runs from west to east to terminate in the corner drawing room, which has magnificent views over the lake and then to the fells beyond. To this narrow end, which also has to take the full force of the Lake District weather at its worst, are arranged a series of garden terraces with a lawn for

The White Drawing Room affords stunning views towards the fells. (© Lakeland Arts)

croquet, and two tennis courts. In *Houses and Gardens*, Baillie Scott wrote that, 'The claims of common sense are paramount in its plan.' The gardens were designed in association with Thomas Mawson (1861–1933), who, together with Gertrude Jekyll, was one of the finest garden designers of the time. In 1900 Mawson published his own influential book entitled *The Art and Craft of Garden Making*. Baillie Scott was also an accomplished garden designer as shown by his collaboration with his friend from Hampstead Garden Suburb days, Charles Paget Wade, on the gardens at Snowshill Manor in Gloucestershire.

Externally the house is dominated by a series of very tall, sharp gables with kneelers. Projecting bays (canted and square) receive the many window seats carefully

dotted around the interior. These also hold Voysey-esque runs of mullioned windows whilst doorheads have just a hint of the Tudor to them. Highly sculptural pairs of tubular chimney stacks – redolent of the local vernacular – break through the simple slate roof, and all is wrapped in a thick, white-painted coat of roughcast to cover the brick construction. Only the limestone dressings of windows and doors are left bare for contrast.

Blackwell came to Baillie Scott not long after he had collaborated with Ashbee and the Guild of Handicraft on the interiors of the ducal palace at Darmstadt. Diane Haigh argues convincingly that this experience persuaded him more than ever on the wisdom of working closely with craftsmen on every aspect of a building, from the furniture and fabrics down to the metalwork and

stained glass. It was also where he began to experiment with the idea of each room as a work of art in its own right. This contrivance is what sets Blackwell apart from many earlier houses of the Arts and Crafts Movement; it was, as

The gardens at Snowshill Manor in the Cotswolds show Baillie Scott's talent as a garden designer.

Only the varying sizes of a standard window design puncture the wrapper of roughcast that gives texture to the garden façade as it rises above the boundary wall.

Muthesius described it, '. . . a new idea of the interior as an autonomous work of art . . . each room is an individual creation, the elements of which spring from the overall idea.' This partly accounts for the character of Blackwell, where mysterious dark wood-panelled corridors give way to halls of great spatial complexity, or lead to bright white rooms that seem to belong to a different building. The effects could be disjointed, disconcerting even, but are handled with such care and sensitivity to their function and location that the visitor is rather transported into the kind of fairy-tale world so often seen in the more exotic Arts and Crafts interiors at their best.

If the planning of the house can be considered to exhibit 'common-sense', the three-dimensional use of interior space is anything but. Mindful of the Lake District weather, the entrance is small, snug, intimate, dark, and womb-like. It is also practical in being draught proof, offering immediate shelter behind its Tudoresque front door, and with a cloakroom and toilet immediately adjacent. And here part of the tactile character of the interior is also established with warm exposed wood panelling, carved Gothic ceiling ribs and bosses, and a wonderfully florid stained-glass window with stylized tulips, designed by Baillie Scott. If the sense of occasion is delayed by this containment, it is immediately rewarded when the door is opened to the cross-passage. The use of materials – oak and stained glass – is carried through but the main feeling is one of being drawn to the light coming in from the south, and through the semi-transparent screen (with sliding doors) to the double-height hall almost in front of one. On entering the hall this clarity is confounded – to the right is the staircase to the bedrooms, which halfway up also diverts via a vaulted stair of its own to another room, almost a minstrels' gallery, above the large inglenook fireplace – effectively a room within a room. As Roderick Gradidge has said, 'This little room is away from the main hall, but is none the less clearly part of it.'[106] The fireplace itself is a beautiful jigsaw puzzle of interlocking green Westmoreland slate and stone. Timber-framed, like the rest of the timbers in the hall, its heavy

Elements of Baillie Scott's work – such as this stained-glass window in the porch – begin to fall over into Art Nouveau. (© Lakeland Arts)

The giant inglenook fireplace in the dining room has fine wood carving to the settle by Arthur Simpson. (© Lakeland Arts)

exposed wooden beams are not merely for decorative effect but are also structural. Vigorous low-relief carving to the panelling, spandrels and brackets are by Arthur Simpson (1857–1922) of Kendal, often depicting the mountain ash trees native to the Lake District. By a happy coincidence they are also part of the Holt family's coat-of-arms, cropping up again and again. To the left as one enters the hall is another aspect of Blackwell's spatial complexity as the architect has carefully slid in a large fixed bench-seat and lowered the ceiling to create a space for a billiard table as part of the expansive open plan.

Beyond the enormous multifunctional living space of the hall lies

The stunning main hall can be opened up by the use of sliding wooden screens yet also allows for intimacy in the 'Minstrels' Gallery' above the fireplace. (© Lakeland Arts)

Rowan trees crop up all over the house – on the battlemented decorative lead rainwater hopper surrounding the owner's initials and date of completion (1900); on the dining-room frieze; and on the plaster frieze in the White Room's inglenook fireplace – a room within a room almost as much as that in the hall. (© Lakeland Arts)

the large, dark, rich dining room, its potential sobriety lifted by the quality of decoration. Here the warm wood panelling continues to envelope the diners but above dado height the walls are covered by hessian printed with rowan, bluebell, and daisy motifs. If the sequence of spaces from hall to dining room, taking in two masterly inglenooks, a billiard room, and minstrels' gallery was not enough, the final surprise is the drawing room to the end of the central corridor. In complete contrast to the varying subtle lighting levels so far, this room is all white, arranged to take full advantage of the views, and flooded with light which bounces off the inset mirrors and the deep blue William De Morgan tiles to the inglenook fireplace. It is, Ian Macdonald-Smith has written, '. . . an exquisite example of opulent restraint.'[107]

# Chapter 6

# Arts and Crafts Spreads Its Wings

THE ARTS AND CRAFTS COMMITMENT TO maintaining, and in many cases reviving, local building traditions can be seen at its best in rural England where it was most at home. However, there was another form of what we would now call regionalism that it championed and that was the invention, or reinvention, of the local vernacular in and around the major manufacturing towns of England. Cities like Birmingham, Manchester, Liverpool, York, Sheffield, Leeds and Newcastle all had their expanding architectural associations and cultural clubs. Here views were exchanged, articles from magazines such as *The Architectural Review* and *The Studio* discussed. All these cities were subject to the same messages coming out of the endeavours of the Arts and Crafts Exhibition Society, Art Workers' Guild, and the campaigning activities of SPAB. And of course, there was no substitute for personal contact. Major figures such as Ruskin, Morris, Lethaby and Crane lectured up and down the country to local groups, often awarding prizes at local art colleges, addressing local businessmen, and extending its influence as they did. But not all responded positively and the spread of the Arts and Crafts Movement was both uneven and unpredictable. Not only was this geographical but also temporal – Arts and Crafts influence can be found not only in odd corners, but also at odd times as it spread across the country.

Usually the regional 'voice' of the Arts and Crafts Movement was embodied in a certain architect, or group of architects, with a shared sensibility and

relationship to their local traditions. Most of these cities still possessed the pre-industrial buildings of merchants and artisans in their city centres, living cheek by jowl with the new architecture of revivalism it emulated. Similarly the suburbs harboured manor houses and rural cottages being gradually engulfed, if not destroyed, by urban expansion. In Manchester, for example, the architect Henry Taylor set about recording some of them in *Old Halls in Lancashire and Cheshire* in 1884 and the Manchester Society of Architects encouraged young trainees to go out into the Pennines to study old buildings and awarded prizes for the best measured drawings. And they were not alone. Up and down the country young architects, enthused by the teachings of Ruskin and Morris, went out to sketch, measure and study the survivals of this unique workaday heritage.

In Sheffield the architect Charles Frederick Innocent wrote early in the twentieth century of the 'strange materials, and curious methods' of building still apparent in the Peak District that sat on the edge of the expanding city and noted that, 'Even now it is possible to travel out of Sheffield on an electric tram-car for a few miles and easily walk to farms where the flail not only hangs behind the barn-door, but is regularly used for threshing.'[108] A whole series of popular books by authors such as Stuart Dick and P.H. Ditchfield, often illustrated by artists such as Helen Allingham, or photographed by W. Galsworthy Davie, were published on the backs of the more serious studies by Neville, Addy, Innocent and others.

Describing an almost lost arcadia, the authors and artists celebrated this fast-disappearing legacy in books of the early twentieth century with titles

Opposite: A simple wooden door latch fashioned out of elm is made 'snowy white' with whitewash at Stoneywell Cottage.

The ragged terrace of weavers' cottages at Arlington Row in Bibury (called by Morris 'the most beautiful village in the country') nestles beneath the greenery of Rack Island, the land where cloth was left to dry.

Perched high above the River Frome sits Pinbury Park at Sapperton. From 1894 it became both the home and the workshops of Ernest Gimson and the brothers Sidney and Ernest Barnsley. Paying £75 a year on a repairing lease to Lord Bathurst, they repaired and adapted both the old farmhouse and a series of outbuildings to become a craft community.

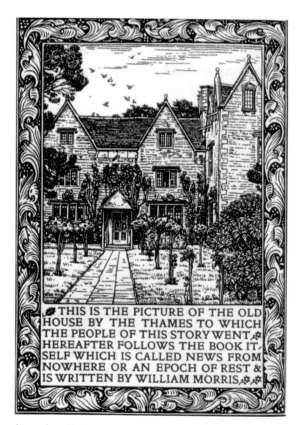

THIS IS THE PICTURE OF THE OLD HOUSE BY THE THAMES TO WHICH THE PEOPLE OF THIS STORY WENT HEREAFTER FOLLOWS THE BOOK IT SELF WHICH IS CALLED NEWS FROM NOWHERE OR AN EPOCH OF REST & IS WRITTEN BY WILLIAM MORRIS

A page from Morris's utopian novel *News from Nowhere* depicting sixteenth-century Kelmscott Manor – which he described as 'heaven on earth' – the family's Cotswold home from 1871. The house gave its name to the Kelmscott Press, which published the book and was created by Morris to revive the art of early printing.

such as *Vanishing England, Rural England, Cottage and Village Life, The Manor-Houses of England* and *The Cottage Homes of England.* The sense of loss was palpable to the Arts and Crafts Movement and in the very teeth of the advanced technology of the day many an architect strove to awake this beauty that had been submerged by 'snorting steam and piston stroke'. Ditchfield paints a picture of how one such technology was viewed by some:

> Now the wayside inns wake up again with the bellow of the motor-car, which like a hideous monster rushes through the old-world villages, startling and killing old slow-footed rustics and scampering children, dogs and hens, and clouds of dust strive in very mercy to hide the view of the terrible rushing demon.[109]

The garden front of Hilles. The prestigious house was designed by, and for, Detmar Blow but his unconventional family life extended to being on almost equal terms with the servants who ran it. Trying to enact Morris's socialism proved to be difficult. At the time it was built Blow was working for the richest man in the country, the Duke of Westminster.

At the centre of Arts and Crafts consciousness was the salving balm represented by the honey-coloured limestone buildings of the Cotswolds. Its impact and influence ran deep – Philip Tilden, for example, admitting of his design for Porth-en-alls in the far west of Cornwall that, 'I wish now that I had kept to the Cornish tradition more closely than I did, but I had been impregnated with the Cotswold tradition . . .'[110] In 1907 Norman Jewson stepped off the train at Cirencester for a holiday in the Cotswolds (and then stayed a lifetime) when it '. . . was little known at that time, except to a few architects and artists who had discovered its fine stone buildings and varied and beautiful scenery.'[111] Foremost amongst these of course was William Morris, who fell in love with its architecture and villages such as the barn at Great Coxwell and Bibury's Arlington Row. Led by the example of Morris putting down roots in Kelmscott Manor, Lethaby and Gimson tried to help Webb find a house to retire to in its deep wooded valleys. Others followed and we have already noted how Gimson and the Barnsley brothers removed themselves to Sapperton to establish their workshops and how Ashbee re-established his Guild of

Handicraft in Chipping Camden. The Sapperton group were soon joined by Alfred Powell (1865–1960), who, together with his wife Ada (1882–1956) extended and built several traditional cottages nearby whilst working both for the group, and themselves. Elsewhere the stained-glass artist Henry Payne established his small St Loe's Guild in Amberley, whilst nearby Powell's close friend and builder colleague, Detmar Blow, built his own towering house Hilles with its commanding views over the River Severn.

Not only was the Cotswolds deep in the movement's consciousness but, and as a result, it was where the movement's ideals of uniting Art and Craft and finding joy in labour were most perfectly realized. Gimson, though trained as an architect and admitting to Lethaby that he thought of architecture 'all the time', developed his skills as a modeller in plasterwork and an accomplished designer-maker in furniture and metal-work. Similarly, Ernest and Sidney Barnsley also began as architects but added other skills, principally furniture making, to their accomplishments.

Sidney is particularly interesting and all too frequently overlooked as an architect. After returning

Once established at Pinbury, Gimson and the Barnsleys also set about designing their own houses nearby. Here we see Leasowes for Ernest Gimson, Beechanger for Sidney Barnsley (both with fanciful dovecotes) and Upper Dorval house for his brother Ernest. Although they sit comfortably in the tradition of Cotswold buildings, Gimson's love of thatch went against the more normal use of the region's plentiful stone slates for roofing.

A gazebo, boundary wall and stone steps act as a domestic gateway to a group of ten cottages, the Gyde Almshouses, in Painswick designed by Ernest Barnsley in 1913. Behind them, and part of the original idea, the enormous Gyde orphanage opened in 1919 – for seventy children aged nine to twelve – and designed by P. Morley Horder in a similar Cotswold manner.

from architectural survey work in Greece with Robert Schultz Weir, he moved to the Cotswolds with his brother and Gimson. Once the workshops were established at Pinbury all three designed their own cottages in Sapperton. Although he never realized the enormous promise suggested by his design of the Church of the Holy Wisdom of God in Lower Kingswood, Surrey (1892), with the exception of a few commissions such as the Gyde Almshouses of 1912–13, following the death of Gimson in 1919 he re-established his architectural career somewhat. This was partly as a clerk of works by completing Gimson's buildings at Bedales, and his brother's work at Rodmarton Manor, but also through a series of workman-like extensions and cottages throughout the Cotswolds such as Talland House, South Cerney (1919–20), Cotswold Farm, Duntisbourne Abbots (1926) and especially the wonderfully understated

Bedales Memorial Library designed by Ernest Gimson comes as a rather unexpected delight after he'd spent much of his career perfecting his skills in wood, metal and especially decorative plasterwork. The exposed blades of the wooden cruck to the porch lead to its accompanying memorial hall. Finished in 1921, two years after Gimson's death, it was completed by Ernest Barnsley and Geoffrey Lupton.

Rodmarton Manor, designed by Ernest Barnsley. Construction of this enormous house (to also be a base for local craft activity) began in 1909 and was worked on by Sidney Barsnley and then Norman Jewson. A vast undertaking, it took twenty-three years to complete and was built only using traditional methods of construction. Rainwater goods are all decorated with animals – this lead hopper (right) is also decorated with one! (Creative Commons Attribution – Share Alike 3.0 Unported (c) Robert Powell)

The builder, and old Bedalian, Geoffrey Lupton, seen guiding one of the library's enormous beams into position using block and tackle. Lupton had trained as a furniture maker under Gimson and commissioned him to design the library and adjacent school hall. (Image courtesy of Bedales)

work in and around Painswick such as Lodge Farm, Sherwood Hill (1923), Little Chapel (1925), Tower Cottage (1926) and even Painswick's public bath-house and attached toilets – possibly with lettering carved by Eric Gill.

## Manchester and the north-west

Whilst the work of the Arts and Crafts Movement in the Cotswolds colours the whole history of the movement, its ideas spread far and wide. Edgar Wood was, by any standard, one of its most remarkable architects and remains greatly under appreciated. Muthesius (who considered he had a 'pervasive poetical overtone') makes the point well in his magisterial survey by writing that, 'It is pleasant to be able to end the list of this largely London-based group of architects with a representative of a similar movement in Manchester, Edgar Wood. Wood is one of the best representatives of those who go their own way and refuse to reproduce earlier styles.'[112] As readily associated with Art Nouveau (like Crane and Mackmurdo) and even (by his more extreme enthusiasts) as being a 'pioneer' of Art Deco, he was one of the leaders of the movement in the north-west of England. His stylized natural motifs and the geometric pattern-making that he so enjoyed suggest such readings. Born and bred in the Lancashire textile town of Middleton, close to Rochdale, the fact that he is considered to have ranged so far across a variety of styles is an indication of his abilities. The son of a wealthy mill owner, it was assumed by his father that the young Edgar would enter the family cotton-spinning business, but he had different ideas and, like his great friend Frederick Jackson (1859–1918), hoped to become a painter. Many a nineteenth-century architect started

with such an ambition but family, and often the religious pressure of the Non-Conformist faith that disapproved of such self-indulgence, encouraged them to channel their ambition into something more 'practical' such as architecture.

Accordingly he served his pupillage under Mills & Murgatroyd of Manchester, a large and reputable architectural practice but not of an Arts and Crafts persuasion. Looking back in 1900 he recalled, 'My earliest architectural years were passed in an atmosphere where beautiful creative powers as applied to building, and life in design generally, were drowned in the solemnity of commerce, tracing paper and the checking of quantities.'[113] After completing his training he established his own practice in Middleton in 1885 and by 1892 was doing so well that he moved to premises in the heart of Manchester and was one of the founders of the Northern Art Workers' Guild in 1896, becoming its Master in 1897. Between 1887 and 1903 he developed a successful practice specializing in housing and church design but with a few interesting commercial buildings, such as a new bank in Middleton. Long Street Methodist Church, Middleton (1899), shows him developing the Gothic language in a stripped-back manner being popularized by other architects of the day such as Temple Moore. The columns of the nave glide effortlessly into their pointed arches uninterrupted by the usual historicist presence of a decorative capital or other element emphasizing the junction and transfer of weight,

A bird's-eye view of the Long Street Methodist Church and Sunday School in Middleton shows Edgar Wood's skill not only as an inventive architect, but as a considerably talented graphic artist. (Courtesy of Manchester Metropolitan Library Special Collections)

A detail of the sparsely elegant stonework of the chapel.

and generally there is a spare and exciting daring to his handling of the stone. Above them curvaceous corbels (their sinuous profile echoed in the design of the bench ends below) project and support an equally inventive wooden trussed roof, which alternates being scissor-braced or hammer-beam from bay to bay. Despite the grounding in historicism of the Gothic the pulpit is a remarkable design, akin to Lethaby's Avon Tyrrell in its realism, whilst the tracery of the east-end window hints at the savageness of Prior or Wells at their best. Wood was Lethaby's kind of architect, and Lethaby Wood's: steeped in tradition but not afraid to step out of it as when he begins experimenting with flat concrete roofs, something Prior and Lethaby had done. Carved into the stone wall are beautifully designed initials of the church's benefactors styled as Byzantine monograms redolent of Lethaby and Swainson's book on *Sancta Sophia*.

This early confidence in working within the local vernacular tradition – but modified by his artistry – is seen in a substantial semi-detached house (although you wouldn't know it to look at it!), perched high above Middleton. This is Redcroft and Fencegate (1885), designed for himself. Compactness and cleverness in the internal planning of his houses was one of his strengths – placing practicality alongside a greatly inventive decorative beauty. By 1890 he had started building in the exclusive new Manchester suburb of Hale with houses such as the red brick and

ashlar Halecroft, a sort of compact Tudor Revival manor house infected with the spirit of the Pre-Raphaelites somewhat akin to Wightwick Manor. Much later, just down the road, he built the remarkable Royd House for himself between 1914 and 1916.

Commissions often came from family and friends. Briar Court, Lindley (1895), designed for his sister Annie and given to her and her husband as a wedding present by his father, the local businessman John Sykes, is one of his finest adaptations of the Pennine vernacular he restyled as his own. Other versions of this model followed – Banney Royd Hall, Huddersfield (1901) and Parsonage House, Thurlstone (1906) being two good, albeit very different, examples. What unites them all is the use of roughly dressed stonewalls, large stone slates for roofing, prominent angular canted bays, often with large mullion and transomed windows (even in a modest row of terraced houses), over-scale dormers and tall bays that puncture eaves lines, and coped gables that speak of the substantial Pennine houses of seventeenth-century Lancashire and the West Riding of Yorkshire

You wouldn't know it to look at it, but this house in Middleton, designed by and for Edgar Wood, is in fact two houses masquerading as one – Fencegate and Redcroft. It's a modern take on Pennine building traditions mixed with symbolism. Wood lived in the section to the left. (© Andy Marshall)

Briar Court of 1908 embodies Wood's approach of mixing historicism, naturalism, and symbolism in his work in pursuit of originality. The bucolic murals were painted by his great friend Frederick Jackson, the stylish doors are in the children's bedroom, and the briar rose plaster frieze in the drawing room. (Courtesy Vicky House)

that he so admired and becomes a recognizable personal language. Once developed it underwent some changes in the speculative work, such as The Shiel (1906), he and similarly minded architects such as John N. Cocker (1883–1960) designed. Found in the Richardson estate in Hale, it forms part of the wonderful late Arts and Crafts suburb.

## Change of direction

Around 1903 Wood's style undergoes a significant change, or maybe is simply added to, as he begins working with James Sellers. Sellers had previously worked with A.J. Penty, one of the movement's most intellectually radical architects, in York. From this date it becomes hard to distinguish Wood from Sellers but the style changes – becoming plainer, more functionalist in appearance, and altogether more structurally inventive. We still need to know more about Wood – a powerfully poetic architect spoken of by Pevsner in the same breath as Gaudi and Mackintosh. Ultimately Wood, and Sellers, perhaps due to their greater exposure to the problems of city living, are better thought of as promoters of the progressive English Free Style. This was a development of the Arts and Crafts Movement which succeeded in freeing itself from the travails of revivalism altogether and which is seen at its best in Wood's most celebrated works such as the First Church of Christ Scientist, Upmeads, and his remarkable schools, rather than the attempt to revivify vernacular architecture which lay at the heart of the Arts and Crafts Movement.

The last house he designed before he retired to Italy to paint, Edgecroft (1921), displays an elegant and gaunt simplicity of handling of brick in common not only with major figures such as Webb and Lethaby but the group of Birmingham architects such as Bidlake, Bateman, and Crouch and Butler, who were exploring the same possibilities for Arts and Crafts architecture.

## Birmingham and the Midlands

Birmingham is said to have had its own Art Workers' Guild around 1902 but little evidence of it exists and it is believed not to have been a success.[114] Alan Crawford in *By Hammer and Hand* argues persuasively that Birmingham had no need for such an organization as it had a variety of active organizations and establishments who fulfilled the educational and exhibition role performed by the guild in London and Manchester. Such was its independent success its architects earned the name of 'the Birmingham group' and even, confusingly, 'the Birmingham School' – confusing as there was a Birmingham School of Art. However, linked to it, and feeding from it, the success of Birmingham's architects and craftsmen went far beyond that of their notable art school.

The Birmingham School of Art headed by Edward R. Taylor, and later Robert Carter-Smith, developed a practical 'learning by doing' philosophy such as lay behind Lethaby's thinking when he established the Central School of Arts and Crafts in London, and the earlier initiative of Ashbee when he established his Guild of Handicraft in Whitechapel. Nor was this the only link between Lethaby and Birmingham. Half of Lethaby's buildings were commissioned directly, or indirectly, by wealthy Birmingham Liberals including

Bournville is a veritable museum of advanced housing design led by W.A. Harvey as seen in this semi-detached chalet bungalow.

The Hurst in Sutton Coldfield, Melsetter House in the Orkneys, and the Eagle Insurance building in Birmingham. He was, together with Morris, a regular guest lecturer at the School of Art, collaborated with Birmingham architect J.L. Ball on the Eagle Insurance building, and through his friendship with the Barnsley brothers (whose father was a prominent local building contractor) was a habitué of the 'city of brick'. Although masters of building in brick, Birmingham's vernacular hinterland possessed some of the finest timber-framed buildings in the country, which were also an inspiration to its receptive young architects. At the new garden village of Bournville on the edge of the city, W.A. Harvey brought all these traditions together to create another Arts and Crafts enclave.

## W.H. Bidlake and his generation

Outwith the spectacular experiment of Bournville, in the architectural fraternity the leading light in Birmingham was W.H. Bidlake (1861–1938). Together with Arthur Dixon, he was at various points a Director of Birmingham's successful Guild of Handicraft in addition to teaching in the School of Art. A skilful church architect from 1889, his style here was a restrained and inventive late Gothic, not dissimilar to contemporaries

Bidlake was very much the leader of the Birmingham School and the Four Oaks estate, where this house is situated, one of the school's great showgrounds. (W. Shaw Sparrow, *The Modern Home*, 1906)

such as Sedding, and Bodley and Garner (whose practice he served part of his articles with). However, it is in domestic design that he showed his real talent; his work, such as Garth House, Edgbaston (1900), and Redcroft (1901) in Four Oaks being praised and illustrated in *The Studio* and by Muthesius in *Das Englische Haus* – as were all of his five houses in Four Oaks. Here he had built his own house, Woodgate, in 1896 (near Lethaby's The Hurst), and whilst his houses of the 1890s retain an echo of their timber-framed vernacular models (such as Wilderhope Manor, Shropshire), by the early 1900s his work progressively sheds overt historic references to delight in what Muthesius praised as 'the plainest of brick walls' – like Edgar Wood. He wrote, 'They are immediately recognisable from their very simple style and the great honesty that they express . . .'[115] The Four Oaks estate boasted work by, amongst others, Reynolds, Hobbiss, Bateman, and Crouch and Butler and, no less than the Richardson estate in Hale, develops a type of suburbia – vernacular rather than Italianate – that became synonymous with the twentieth century. Crouch, in his own house, Seven Gables in Sutton Coldfield, shows his own preference for a half-timbered Domestic Revival, yet Avon Croft of 1900 on the Four Oaks estate sees the revivalist tendency modified by a thick coat of Voysey-esque roughcast porridge. Like other Birmingham architects the firm often employed the Bromsgrove Guild artists to decorate their interiors, including work by Benjamin Creswick, the Sheffield modeller Ruskin plucked from obscurity.

Although it still attracts an all too easy sneer, the suburb of the late nineteenth and early twentieth century (as envisaged by the Arts and Crafts Movement) should be valued for creating a healthy and attractive alternative to cramped and insanitary inner-city developments. We see it at its finest in Birmingham.

Where Bidlake led, his talented colleagues followed. J.L. Ball at Furze Hill, near Broadway (a butterfly plan house of 1900) and most assuredly Winterbourne (1902–04), in Edgbaston, show why he is said to have nearly gone into partnership with

'Redlands' by Charles Bateman – another tour de force in brick on Sutton Coldfield's Four Oaks estate where over 200 houses were built between 1895 and 1914. (W. Shaw Sparrow, *The Modern Home*, 1906)

Lethaby (whose High Coxlease it has remarkable stylistic affinities with). Charles Bateman (1863–1947), the middle of three generations of Birmingham architects, was perhaps more liberally minded than Bidlake and Ball in his acceptance of historicism, and so, like Reginald Blomfield or Ernest Newton, could, and did, turn his hand to a variety of Free Renaissance and quasi-vernacular styles which may question his commitment to the Arts and Crafts Movement. Yet in houses such as The Homestead (1896), Edgbaston, he displays a Voysey-like assurance in creating the new style – but seen as style rather than commitment. What is true of Bateman may also be true of Crouch and Butler but cannot and should not be applied to the more advanced work of Buckland and Farmer and particularly A.S. Dixon.

## York and Yorkshire

York, although now mainly thought of as a great medieval city, was, in the nineteenth century, synonymous with industry and one industry in particular: the railways. The resulting housing problems, famously highlighted by the Quaker Rowntree family of York, led to significant early experiments in the design of good-quality low-cost housing no less than the Cadbury family instigated at Bournville. At New Earswick, begun on the outskirts of York in 1904, the confectioner Joseph Rowntree (1836–1925) created a model village of short terraces, laid out in a seemingly random, irregular pattern, conforming to a village-like ideal to house his workers interspersed with communal facilities such as its Folk Hall. Designed by Parker and Unwin, they demonstrated what was possible when industrialists with a social conscience, like the Cadburys at Bournville, were engaged. Joseph had also been amongst the first major employers to instigate occupational pension schemes for the employees in his chocolate factory. It was Joseph's son, Seebohm Rowntree (1871–1954), who went further in the fight for good-quality housing by undertaking one of the earliest social surveys of poverty and whose reports became one of the foundations of the future Welfare State. Intriguingly a slight relation, Fred Rowntree (1860–1927), became a member of the Art Workers' Guild in 1907 and practised as an architect in Yorkshire with houses in Scarborough and the surrounding area before relocating to London and Scotland. Indeed Scarborough boasted several good architects alongside Rowntree. Despite this relocation to Scotland, the Quaker connection proved important as in 1919 work began on the ambitious Jordans village in Buckinghamshire to a plan, and housing, designed by Fred Rowntree. An extension of the seventeenth-century Old Jordans village, not only was it designed along Arts and Crafts lines but a philanthropic company was established, Jordan Village Industries Ltd., which created the materials – bricks, ironwork, and so on – to build it. One of the many idealistic attempts to maintain the pre-war ideals of the Garden City Movement and the idea of the craft village, the Industries closed in 1923 as most of the housing was completed. At the same time Fred and his partner W.J. Swain were employed to design York's first municipal park, Rowntree Park, laid out between 1919 and 1921 along Arts and Crafts lines.

## The movement with a sweet tooth – Walter Brierley in York

The Arts and Crafts Movement seemed to have an extraordinary affinity with chocolate – indeed it seems to have had something of a sweet tooth. Running a close second to railways and engineering, York also boasted two major confectionery manufacturers – Terry's chocolate empire, as well as Rowntree's – as major employers. And it was the Terry family, in the shape of Noel Terry, that commissioned one of the movement's most celebrated houses in York – Goddards.

The last building designed by Walter Brierley (1862–1926), like Edgar Wood in Manchester and Lancashire he spent his entire working life (of forty years) associated with his region – in this case York and Yorkshire – to the extent that he stands for the Arts and Crafts Movement in this area. A measure of his talent as a designer may be judged from the accolade of often being referred to as 'the Yorkshire Lutyens' or even the 'Lutyens of the North'. To cement the association with Lutyens, his own house of 1905, Bishopbarns, had its gardens designed by Gertrude Jekyll. Another master of brick detailing like the 'Birmingham School', but here more often hand-made brick, he was also liberal in his attitude to style and as readily embraces the 'Wrenaissance', or late Gothic, as he does the Arts and Crafts vernacular. So for Brierley it seems the movement was more about a fashionable style than a commitment to social justice and 'joy in labour'. A million miles away from the concern for the craftsman exhibited by Webb, Brierley is reputed to have savagely upbraided his workmen for not following his instructions to the letter – no room for glorying in Ruskinian imperfection for him! So the results, judged by Goddards, or his own house in York, Bishopbarns, are persuasive of an understanding of the delight to be found in designing a well-detailed building. Whilst there is no doubting his inventiveness or talent, he is more an architect of continuity than change. Where a progressive spirit may be seen is in his schools for the York School Board, and particularly the very Webbian Scarcroft

Goddards in York was designed for Noel Terry, the chocolate heir, by the county's leading Arts and Crafts architect, Walter Brierley – sometimes referred to as 'the Lutyens of the North'.

York's Scarcroft Road School is considered Brierley's best work – it combines good planning with a progressive interpretation of Gothic and early Renaissance architecture reminiscent of Webb.

Road School, York. Many an architect had reason to be grateful for the expansion of primary education following Forster's Education Act in 1870. Brierley was not only the salaried architect to the York School Board but in 1899 he was commissioned to design a house for the headmaster of the Yorkshire School for the Blind – a well-endowed charitable foundation built in the centre of York – to blend in with the medieval King's Manor. Here he shows lessons learnt from Devey in adding 'instant heritage' by mixing up materials in a seemingly random way suggestive of a rebuilding, and in his largely speculative work in Goathland in its cottages and Mallan Hotel. Across the Pennines from Yorkshire, in Accrington, stands Brierley's Hollins Hill (now the Haworth Art Gallery) of 1908–09 – showing his versatility and handling of regional variation. A stunning essay in Pennine manor house architecture, it could be by Edgar Wood but for its lack of inventive decoration.

Finally in York, although he stayed in the city very

The patchwork pattern of materials on the headmaster's house tries to suggest a building that has grown up over time. It was actually brand new in 1899.

**Porth-en-Alls, Cornwall, East Front,** PHILIP A. TILDEN, Architect.
*Hope's Casements.*

little, mention must be made of A.J. Penty, perhaps best known as the designer of the very accomplished and prepossessing blocks of flats at Temple Fortune, which suggest an entrance into Hampstead Garden Suburb. Penty was the elder of two architect sons of W.G. Penty of York. Trained in his father's office, and later made a partner, amongst his works in York before he moved to London in 1902 he designed two houses for local businessmen, Aldersyde and Elmbank (now a hotel), and the Four Alls Inn. By the time he moved to London, where he met up with Fred Rowntree to form a furniture-making company not dissimilar to Kenton & Co. (with fellow architect Charles Spooner), he was also establishing a reputation as a radical thinker. In 1903, together with Alfred R. Orage and Holbrook Jackson, he established the Leeds City Art Club which promoted radical ideas and Penty, by now a member of the Fabian Society and active in socialist politics, developed a branch of Guild Socialism – a form of organization which advocated workers' control of the means of production as outlined in his book of 1906, *The Restoration*

Porth-en-Alls sits perilously close to the sea in Cornwall's Prussia Cove. The drawing (from *Academy Architecture,* 1912) shows how the architect hoped to complete it, 'but I had to content myself with half a dream come true…'. The curvaceous cottage replaces that lived in by the infamous smuggler, the 'King of Prussia'.

*of the Gild System* where, enthralled by Morris and with affinities to Mackmurdo's similar radicalism, he advocated a return to workshop production based on the medieval guild and the end of the factories system.

## Working in splendid isolation

Many other cities boasted individual architects of talent caught up in the heady ideas of the 1880s and 1890s even if they failed to either speak with a common voice or form a cohesive group. Of course in such cases it may well be that the client was more forceful in having what they wanted than the architect was in opposing them. Additionally the often slower rate of assimilation of Arts and Crafts ideas away from the major intellectual centres also slowed down progress in certain pockets of the country. But for all that, the provinces were often far from provincial in their outlook and can contain surprises.

Sheffield, dominated by the metal industries no less than Birmingham, might have seemed an obvious breeding ground, especially with the encouragement of Ruskin establishing an outpost of his St George's Guild there in 1875. Yet beyond the few examples of work by C.F. Innocent (including in the very forward-thinking Flower estate at Wincobank established by the Sheffield Corporation as early as 1900), W.J. Hale (1862–1929) and most of all Norman Doncaster's accomplished Moorwinstow (1912), it is a little disappointing. Rather its significant contribution was more in the field of scholarship and the rediscovery of vernacular building methods – those 'strange materials and curious methods'. Likewise Liverpool and Newcastle, though they both boast great craftsmanship. Yet Newcastle, even boasting such considerable talents as Yorkshire-born Frank W. Rich (1840–1929) and Robert Burns Dick (1868–1954), failed to achieve any more particular stature than its northern neighbour Carlisle and, like Liverpool, seems to miss out the Arts and Crafts Movement in preference to a robust Art Nouveau. Leicester, had Gimson stayed rather than be seduced by Morris to abandon his home town in favour of London and the office of Sedding, displayed promise and in the White House in Leicester of 1897 (designed over a decade after he left the city) he shows what might have been had he stayed.

United by its almost complete drenching in grey slate, the overall composition of Trevelloe also seems to owe something to a construction game for children that the architect designed.

Whilst Cornwall cannot boast of any great indigenous Arts and Crafts architects the growth of the Newlyn School of painting, centred on the artist Stanhope Forbes, created a culture as receptive to its ideas as was its landscape. The work of two architects stands out. Firstly the chimeral Philip Tilden who was asked to dramatically remodel and extend a magnificently sited, but poorly designed, new house in Prussia Cove, or as he put it, '. . . destroying as much of this new usurper as I could, and hiding what I could not destroy.'[116] This was Porth-en-Alls of 1911. Two years later he exhibited similarly imaginative additions to nearby Godolphin House.

Secondly, Arnold Mitchell. Mitchell, whose own house, Sundial Cottage, in Lyme Regis on Dorset's Jurassic coast is so related to the local geography that it includes ammonites in its walls, designed two buildings of note near Penzance. Firstly, the partially slate-clad Wheal Betsy (1909) for the painter Thomas Gotch, and secondly the totally slate-clad Trevelloe (1911) in the nearby Lamorna Valley for W.T. Bolitho. Both delight in slate and granite – the materials that define this landscape.

This has not been a comprehensive tour of the country and thankfully there remain many other architects and buildings of the Arts and Crafts Movement to be enjoyed.

Stoneywell seems to almost fall down the hillside it grows out of.

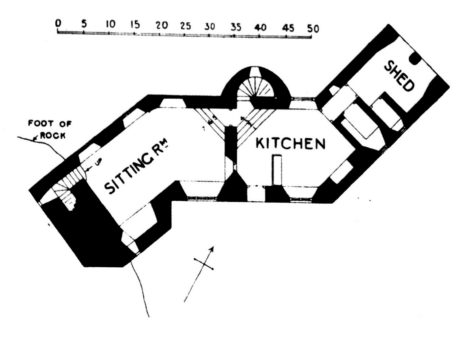

Stoneywell Cottage, Ulverscroft, Leicestershire (1898–99) is one of the most quintessential, if not extreme, buildings of the Arts and Crafts Movement. Extreme in its simplicity, its relation to the landscape, and in its adherence to the ideas of the movement. If there is one building above all others that stands for its ideals, it is this one. Although designed by Gimson for his brother, Sydney, it was a collaborative endeavour with architect, client, clerk of works and builder contributing to the overall design and construction as a collaborative exercise. This was partly dictated by ideology, but partly by practicality enabled by such an ideology.

Gimson, although born and bred locally in Leicester, was by 1898 living in faraway Gloucestershire. By this stage he had already formed a close working relationship with his builder, Detmar Blow, and his sometime clerk of works, Alfred Powell. In essence all three acted as clerk of works to oversee the construction as, and when, they could. Annoyingly for the client, Blow was working on other jobs at the same time – but then so was Gimson. Nonetheless the two collaborated over the next twenty years, Blow becoming a near neighbour of Gimson in building Hilles, and Powell also moved to the Cotswolds within a few years. Just as Gimson asked Powell to work on Stoneywell for him, so he was working for Powell in Surrey on Long Copse – a long,

The artist G.F. Watts called Long Copse 'the most beautiful house in Surrey'. (Lawrence Weaver, *Small Country Houses of To-day*, 1922)

Gimson's use of running vines, rambling roses, oak leaves and acorns were favourite natural motifs as seen here on the lead gutters.

low, thatched cottage with winding stair-turret, which has clear affinities with Stoneywell. Stoneywell's materials – stone, timber, thatch, lead – are honestly, almost brazenly, expressed and seem to be barely processed – stone dug on site, bound together with lime mortar mixed with granite dust from the same stone, timber rudely dressed for the exposed roof beams, local thatch uniting the carefully balanced yet functionally placed series of dormer windows, lintels left powerfully exposed. Unsettlingly vernacular, the critic Lawrence Weaver, a great admirer of Gimson's work at Sapperton, called Stoneywell 'an unusual product of the building art'.

Ernest was the son of Josiah Gimson, the founder of a successful engineering firm in Leicester. Amongst their works were the engines for the Abbey Pumping Station still in operation today. A member of the Secular Society, the young Ernest was training to be an architect and serving his articles under the Leicester architect Isaac Barradale and supplementing this practical training, as was usual, by attending classes at the local art college. However, in 1884 William Morris came to give a lecture to the Secular Society and everything changed for the young nineteen-year-old trainee architect. Staying with the family after the lecture, Morris and Gimson talked till the early hours. The older man, recognizing Gimson's potential, advised him to leave Leicester and gave him three letters of introduction to well-known London architects. It may be no coincidence that he ended up working for Sedding, whose office was next door to the Morris & Co. showrooms on Oxford Street in London.

As we've already seen, Sedding's office, together with that of Richard Norman Shaw, was one of the two great seed-beds of the Arts and Crafts Movement in

London, particularly for architecture. During the two years he worked for Sedding, 1886–88, he'd have met Sedding's chief assistant, the poetic Henry Wilson, and his future life-long collaborators Alfred Powell and the brothers Sidney and Ernest Barnsley and eventually shared lodgings with Sidney Barnsley, who worked in Shaw's office. Links between the two offices were all the closer as Lethaby, Shaw's chief assistant, and Henry Wilson, were close friends. As Gimson and the Barnsleys' friendship grew they took an office next to that of their revered Webb in Raymond Buildings, Gray's Inn, to become part of what they all jokingly referred to as 'the Square circle'.

Gimson was clearly receptive to the ideals of the Arts and Crafts Movement and would have gained much from his contact with Sedding, who wrote, 'The real architect of a building . . . must be his own clerk of works, his own carver, his own director, he must be the familiar spirit of the structure as it rises from the ground... to make the most of the site and the building as applied to it.'[117]

This could almost be a prescription for the design of Stoneywell. Like so many significant buildings of the movement it was built as a holiday home. Sydney Gimson lived and worked in Leicester, about ten miles north-west of the city, where he was the director

The unyielding stone of the Charnwood Forest is what gives the cottage its character.

of the family's Vulcan Works. In the 1870s he and family friends had often walked, camped and cycled in the sixty square miles of Charnwood Forest's remote, austere, gorse-covered and rocky landscape. These rocks, many pre-Cambrian and so amongst the oldest on the planet, give the landscape a wild and abandoned character that clearly appealed to the Gimsons. Norman Jewson, who built Rockyfield, the last of the group in Charnwood by Gimson, described it on one of his visits: 'The Charnwood Forest is a great tract of primitive woodland country, in which are several disused slate quarries which have become picturesque lakes, with steep rocky sides formed of the beautiful many coloured slates of the district . . .'[118]

In the early 1890s Sydney bought land in the forest for three

Four of the seven steps that link the kitchen to the sitting room, as the building climbs the landscape. But for the exposed polished elm, everything is covered in a thick coat of whitewash.

The enormous chimney stack seems to almost tether the cottage to the site.

cottages: one for himself, one for his older brother Mentor and a third for a friend, Leicester businessmen James Billson, already living nearby in Chitterman Hills Farm. Ernest was commissioned to design a house for each of them, starting with a semi-detached cottage for Billson in 1897. Stoneywell is thus one of four cottages designed by Gimson at Ulverscroft between 1897 and 1908 that form a powerful group of Arts and Crafts architecture.

By this date, captivated by the lectures and demonstrations he had seen at the Art Workers' Guild, Ernest had decided to become a craftsman as much as an architect and by 1893, together with the Barnsley brothers, had moved to Sapperton in rural Gloucestershire to set up a workshop. Imbued with the ideals of Morris and Ruskin, and perhaps his training under Sedding (whom he fell out with) he became the most austere and dedicated of Arts and Crafts architects. One of the beauties of Stoneywell – named after the section of forest closest to the building – is that not only was it designed by Gimson but it was equipped with furniture and fittings made, and supplied, by Gimson and the Barnsleys from their workshops in Gloucestershire. The nineteen items they supplied included a large settle designed by Ernest Barnsley, originally placed near the porchless kitchen door (the only way in) to act as a windbreak – Gimson seeing the porch as a waste of space.

The client – his brother – selected the site he wanted based on his own familiarity with the area and picked his favourite spot. Nonetheless Ernest persuaded him to change sites, and even buy back an extra strip of land from Billson to allow it. On approaching the house it seems to be half-buried in the landscape as it cascades down from bedroom to kitchen. The roof was originally covered with local thatch – the thatcher being brought in from Oxfordshire. Beneath this the particular nature of the site allowed, or suggested, the irregular zig-zag or double-cranked plan as Gimson took advantage of the outcrops of rock for foundations. A conventional approach would have been to have found level ground or, if that wasn't possible, to have levelled the site to start with. Ironically this happened later when Sydney, a keen tennis player, blasted part of the site level to make a tennis court. Gimson shows himself to be working with nature to the extent that in places the stone outcrops merge with the random rubble walls almost seamlessly. As Peter Davey has remarked, 'If nature made buildings, they would surely look something like Stoneywell.'[119]

Once inside, the house pivots on its steps from one room to the next – seven broad steps being necessary to move between kitchen and sitting room (surprisingly there are only two rooms apart from the bedrooms) and six changes of level are encountered from the bottom to the top of the house. Once there, in the 'Olympus' bedroom as it was jokingly called, it was possible to step through the window onto flat land. Indeed the plan seems to slowly meander up (or slide down) the hill in a way that gently emulates the movement of the grazing sheep passing the front door.

The magnificently rugged and primitive chimney stack, one of the most iconic images of the architecture of the Arts and Crafts Movement since Gimson's friend F.L. Griggs drew it for Lethaby's biography of him, acts as an enormous stake fixing the cottage to the ground and seemingly extending the natural outcrop it is built on into the sky. As Michael Drury has commented, '. . . it is hard tell where the outcrop ends and the massive chimney begins.'[120] Not without precedent, as with any vernacular building, it is nonetheless perhaps a knowing reference back to the chimney stacks at the Old Post Office, Tintagel for Blow, who had repaired the building for SPAB. To the rear elevation, another Tintagel reference, is the expressed stair which further counteracts the lateral movement of the façade, and holds some of its articulated parts together. The Old Post Office – an early acquisition of the National Trust – was close to Tintagel Castle and becoming a favoured cottage-type of building admired not merely

As if to emphasize their size the enormous slate lintels are left uncovered as a feature in the wall.

for its vernacular qualities but for its association with medieval and Arthurian myth – Tintagel being one of the supposed sites of Camelot.

Clearly the organic character of the house was greatly aided by Gimson's choice of Blow as clerk of works, or site supervisor. Blow had trained as an architect in London, having been articled to a practice called Wilson and Aldwinckle. This training he supplemented with attendance at the South Kensington School – where incidentally he met and

befriended the shy Lutyens. As a result of winning the Architectural Association's Travelling Scholarship in 1889 he came under Ruskin's direct influence on his travels. On his return he demonstrated Ruskin's influence by apprenticing himself to a traditional builder in Newcastle-Upon-Tyne and effectively retrained as a stonemason to become more of a journeyman, or wandering architect.

After this retraining Blow left Newcastle to work on buildings for SPAB under Webb's direction and for Hugh Fairfax-Cholmeley in North Yorkshire, especially Mill Hill, and other buildings in the estate village of Brandsby. With the team of masons he'd built up during these years, by the time of Stoneywell he was able to provide the kind of direct labour that Gimson wanted. Although they opened up a quarry on the site, much of the stone was also found lying on the surface or just beneath. Careful stone selection reduced the need for dressing the stones (a hard job given their igneous characteristics), which were roughly laid to create a stable but undulating surface externally. Where a particular slate projected out near the sitting room fireplace, Blow advised keeping it to form a shelf – and it was used by Sydney Gimson to keep his tobacco jar on. Inside unity, simplicity and lightness was created by whitewashing everything to an almost puritanical plainness but against which the natural colours of the furnishings show up well.

Particularly impressive are the large exposed slate lintels selected by Blow – one to the front door, the other to the kitchen fireplace. As Weaver noted when he visited Stoneywell, 'The lintel over the fireplace is an amazing bit of construction, a single gigantic slab weighing a ton and a half, a rough shard of slate that had lain neglected in an old quarry until Mr Detmar Blow spied it.'[121] Elsewhere, in typically cavalier style, Blow was not averse to 'accidentally' backing a cart into a local stone wall containing a stone he admired, then replacing the stone with others. Gimson suffered some anxiety as a result of the traditional lime mortar he used in preference to quick-setting ordinary Portland cement, but the local mason is reported to have assured him with the words, 'Don't you be uneasy Sir. It'll be right enough when the warm weather comes along.'[122] And it was. Perhaps the greatest accolade for Stoneywell is the

story that a former local who returned after it had been built was disorientated because he couldn't remember it.

The cottage cost £920 to build – nearly twice what his brother hoped – and underwent various changes in the course of family ownership. Thankfully this was not an experiment in trying to keep costs down as with the 'Cheap Cottage Exhibition' at Letchworth Garden City in 1902 where the target was £150. However, costs were kept to a minimum by for example using chestnut instead of oak for floors, doors and even the door latches, and the Sapperton workshops supplying other details such as the metalwork. The final word should perhaps go to Weaver who wrote, 'Stoneywell cottage has been roughly, even rudely, built, but no tool has been lifted to mark a false impression of age.'[123]

All the metalwork and furniture came from Gimson and the Barnsleys' workshops in Sapperton.

Oak leaves and acorns proliferate in this beautiful detail of a candle sconce designed by Gimson.

# Chapter 7

# The Garden City Movement – Arts and Crafts For All?

I T IS FITTING TO CLOSE THIS BOOK BY LOOKING at the Garden City Movement and how the Arts and Crafts pursuit of the simple life came to influence great swathes of the country's housing. No less than 'Arts' and 'Crafts', by putting the two opposite concepts of 'Garden' and 'City' together in one memorable phrase, people began to think about the issues in a new way.

The last decade of the nineteenth century – beginning with the Housing of the Working Classes Act of 1890 – and the first decade of the twentieth – ending with the first international conference on planning held in London in 1910 – witnessed a series of remarkable changes in the design, layout and provision of mass housing growing out of the Garden City Movement. In many respects this utopian movement shared the backward glance of Morris and his exhortation to 'forget six counties overhung with smoke . . . and the spreading of the hideous town'. In place of industrial England, the Garden City Movement created a nostalgic vision of a pre-industrial village life adapted to the twentieth century. Bibury, with its picturesque weavers' cottages on Arlington Row, was described by Morris as 'the most beautiful village in England' and it's easy to see why. Yet too often criticism of the Arts and Crafts Movement has been that it was too idealistic and utopian and took refuge in a nostalgic view of a rural past, which had all but disappeared. That rather than coping with change it simply turned its back on the problems of contemporary living and preferred a medieval-inspired

Opposite: A simple wooden garden gate sets the suburban tone in Hampstead Garden Suburb.

*Illus. 97.—An imaginary irregular town.*

An imaginary village drawn by C.P. Wade is one of many bucolic images offered in Unwin's *Town Planning in Practice*, showing the ideal being searched for. (Raymond Unwin, *Town Planning in Practice*, 1909)

dream-like world that only the wealthy could afford. The success of the Garden City Movement and its influence gives the lie to this view.

In 1894, Morris gave a speech to an audience in Ancoats, Manchester, on the topic of 'Makeshift' and asked them to:

. . . contrast such monstrosities of haphazard growth as your Manchester-Salford-Oldham etc., or our great sprawling brick and mortar country of London, with what a city might be; the centre with its big public buildings, theatres, squares and gardens: the zone round the centre with its lesser guildhalls grouping together the houses of the citizens; again with its parks and gardens; the outer zone again, still its district of public buildings, but with no definite gardens to it because the whole of this outer zone would be a garden thickly besprinkled with houses and other buildings. And at last the suburb proper, mostly fields and fruit gardens with scanty houses dotted about till you come to the open country with its occasional farm-steads. There would be a city for you.[124]

This is worth quoting at length because what is so very interesting about Morris's utopian vision here is how close it is to what actually happened.

In simple visual terms, garden cities were as he describes. A city centre composed of public buildings set amongst formal parks and radiating avenues; then a smattering of large houses with gardens laid out in a somewhat random and relaxed pattern as if they had grown up over time. Beyond this a further mingling of public buildings and smaller houses all enmeshed in parks and gardens, with agriculture and industry to the edge and served by the railway – the balance of the built and the unbuilt being essential to create a low-density city with fresh air and green spaces – as if a city had been built in a garden. The celebratory tone he gives to the phrase 'at last the suburb proper', spoken as if the town itself was something to escape from to a semi-rural paradise, is very telling. This is also somewhat ironic now as for much of the last century the suburbs, and suburbia generally, amongst many intellectuals and architects was seen as wasteful of land, too rigidly middle-class in its composition, architecturally dreary, and politically conservative.

## Nineteenth-century housing and the development of planning

The overriding problem for housing was the location of work, the cost of providing the workers'

accommodation nearby, and how private enterprise could provide good housing at affordable rents and yet make a profit. These problems had become more and more apparent during the eighteenth and nineteenth centuries when factory labour was established first in the 'dark Satanic mills' of Manchester, Leeds and elsewhere so that by 1851 the census revealed that over half of the population were living in towns for the first time.

Planning, as we understand it today, was in its infancy in the late nineteenth century. Concerned with trying to ameliorate the unplanned and unregulated urban expansion caused by industrialization, this was the 'makeshift' landscape that Morris railed against. In its place was wanted planned growth, good standards of housing and hygiene, and a sense of community. The expensive part of any new housing development was the cost of the land and then road and sewer construction. Whilst standards were laid down for this in local bye-laws, they did not extend to the more detailed design of the housing. It followed that for those seeking to make money by building houses for rent, the more that could be crammed onto a street the greater the profit would be. Accordingly, high densities of up to forty houses per acre were not uncommon, and the houses were usually in multiple occupation, with cellar dwellings commonplace, all laid out to a monotonous grid pattern of densely packed identical streets. Such areas of housing became known as bye-law housing. However, with the introduction of the 'Housing of the Working Classes Act' in 1890 local councils could not only condemn slum dwellings but also buy land for constructing new housing to higher standards. Significant as this interference in the free market was, only a few of the major cities such as London, Liverpool, Glasgow and Sheffield took up the provisions of the act. Whilst philanthropic organizations such as the Peabody Trust, the Improved Industrial Dwellings Company, and the Artizans, Labourers and General Dwellings Company (all established in the 1860s) did much to try and provide decent housing for the least well off, usually in the form of well-designed

Unwin contrasts two systems of development in *Nothing Gained by Overcrowding,* published in 1912.

TWO SYSTEMS OF DEVELOPMENT CONTRASTED

tenements, it was small-scale and what was ultimately needed was concerted government action to solve the housing problems caused by industrialization.

## The Bedford Park estate, London

One of the earliest attempts to oppose the dreariness of nineteenth-century housing and, as Morris wrote, 'turn this land from a grimy back yard of a workshop into a garden' can be seen in Bedford Park. Built between 1875 and 1886 by the developer Jonathan Carr and often, inaccurately, called the world's first purpose-designed garden suburb, Bedford Park is important for setting new standards of suburban development and fixing part of its future character.

Created for the increasingly powerful middle class in 1875, Carr bought twenty-four acres of land near the recently opened Turnham Green station and began to build spaciously distributed houses with gardens set amongst the mature trees on the site. Although its housing was originally designed by the fashionable architects of the Aesthetic Movement, E.W. Godwin, and then Coe & Robinson, in 1877 Carr commissioned Richard Norman Shaw to complete the bulk of the housing. Shaw designed not only much of the housing, including modest pairs of semi-detached

houses, but the other buildings necessary for a suburb to thrive including a church, shops, pub, and even an art school. Whilst the layout of the estate was already determined, Shaw had a pretty free hand to design the houses in the newly fashionable 'Queen Anne' style he had made his own whilst adhering to a set number of standard house-types to maintain Carr's costs. Within these constraints the mixture of detached, semi-detached, and short terraces of housing delights in historic details drawn from Dutch domestic architecture and seventeenth-century architecture generally. These included curved and crow-stepped gables, broken pediments, elaborate white-painted porches and door-hoods, balconies and woodwork, a varied and inventive use of brick (often two different tones of red or brown), rubbed and gauged brickwork, tile-hanging, pargetting, render, bastardized Classical details, and exaggerated multi-paned bay windows and elongated chimney stacks, and all set in delightful gardens. The estate's distinctive and eclectic architecture was continued by Maurice Adams and E.J. May. The variety of detail ensured the houses were a million miles away from the restrained stuccoed early nineteenth-century villas of St John's Wood and Park Village in Regent's Park, which had typified such developments previously and were associated with the upper classes. The area quickly became seen as

Festoons on gables, projecting wooden balconies, two-tones (and shapes) of red tiles, small-paned casement windows and barge boards, amidst white-painted roughcast all contrive to create a scenography beauty amidst the trees of the estate.

A terrace of Queen Anne houses in Bedford Park shows how artistry could transform the terrace by, in this example, looking to early Renaissance Dutch architecture.

an aesthete's paradise to the extent that many houses were built with artists' studios and the estate soon boasted artistic residents. One such was J.W. Foster, for whom Voysey designed the distinctive studio house at 14, South Parade in 1890, better known as the White House, designed as something of a criticism of the dominant red brick of Bedford Park. When reviewed by *The Studio* magazine in 1897

When first completed in 1891, Voysey's White House on South Parade was a refined slap in the face to Bedford Park's gauche Queen Annery to the extent that the builders had to be persuaded that this is what it was meant to look like. Note the elegance of the slim, curving gutter brackets.

they commented that; 'It is amusing to read that it was found necessary, in order to prevent the builder from displaying the usual "ovolo mouldings", "stop chamfers", "fillets" and the like, to prepare eighteen sheets of contract drawings to show where his beloved ornamentation was to be omitted.'

## Model industrial villages

Before the advent of the garden city proper, the idea of a better way of living along the lines suggested by Morris, and Bedford Park, was also being taken up in a series of model industrial villages. Built for wealthy industrialists – William Lever, George Cadbury and Joseph Rowntree – they were Port Sunlight, Bournville and New Earswick respectively and all developed just as the Arts and Crafts Movement was developing in the late 1880s and 1890s.

### Port Sunlight

Port Sunlight began in 1888 – in other words just as Bedford Park was nearing completion – and its founder William Lever (later Lord Leverhulme) claimed that he wanted Port Sunlight 'to socialise and Christianise business relations and get back to that close family brotherhood that existed in the good old days of hand labour.'[125] It was a hugely ambitious undertaking, with 800 houses built between 1899 and 1914 to a very low density of seven houses per acre. Named after the Lever Brothers' most popular brand of soap, Port Sunlight's fifty-six-acre site boasted a great variety of housing, and an unusual layout due to being built on marshy land with a varied topography and housing designed by thirty different architects. At the heart of the housing a muddy inlet was drained, transformed into a garden walk, and renamed The Dell. It was a difficult and inhospitable site but working with its uneven surface and creeks created just the sort of informal random grouping of buildings suggestive of an organic development

William Hesketh Lever was probably something of a frustrated architect and employed some of the best architects in the country to design a variety of different housing types for his workforce at Port Sunlight in Cheshire.

over time that was increasingly favoured. No less than Devey or Webb's approach to architecture as creating an 'instant heritage', the layout of buildings at Port Sunlight suggested a time-honoured community which had grown over the centuries, each age adding another layer of history despite being new. This impression was aided greatly by the design of the housing itself by many of the leading practitioners of the day such as Maurice Adams (fresh from Bedford Park), Edwin Lutyens, Ernest George and Yeates, and Ernest Newton.

Lever – who took a hand in selecting all the architects employed – was a great supporter of the arts generally and counted many architects and artists amongst his friends. Some of the earliest houses at Port Sunlight were designed by his friend William

Set back from the road to allow more open space, this large block of housing is carefully unified into a single composition.

W.A. Harvey understood Birmingham's strong tradition of building in brick and used it well in Bournville for the Cadbury workforce.

Owen (and his son William Segar Owen). Other local architects of note included John Douglas, T.M. Lockwood, Grayson and Ould, Maxwell and Tuke, and J.J. Talbot. Individual houses were grouped by good design into large blocks with unifying facades and set around the edge of plots with spacious lawns and gardens to the front, and allotments and other communal facilities hidden to the rear. Not only did Lever supply subsidized housing for his workers but separate canteens for male and female workers, a school, a technical institute, a cottage hospital, clubs, and a Congregational church.

Beyond its comprehensiveness and ambition Port Sunlight represented the meeting of two different approaches to estate layout. Initially the village was developed in the native picturesque tradition seen at Bedford Park of meandering curving roads with housing set back in a varied building line to suggest something of a village that had grown up over centuries. In this regard the more meticulously revivalist character of some of the houses, especially those reminiscent of the traditions of local half-timbering, reinforced this impression. But later Lever became interested in the latest American ideas on planning, the 'City Beautiful Movement' and the concept of parkways. To ensure wider adoption of these ideas he went on to fund the new Department of Civic Design at Liverpool University. The later stages of development therefore introduced wide, straight vistas with major buildings, such as the Lady Lever Art Gallery, at key axis points and laid a framework of urban and ceremonial formality over the informal picturesque Arts and Crafts village layout.

Overall to walk around Port Sunlight, then as now, is

to be in the enthralling death throes of nineteenth-century revivalism. One might even call it a museum of revivalism. Here we have Dutch, French, Tudor, Renaissance and even Gothic housing blocks. It produces a wonderful variety and a stimulating experience but has no stylistic integrity and feels as unworldly and as embedded in fantasy as Bedford Park. It was a philanthropic showpiece by a philanthropic showman. Lever was an adept businessman albeit with a sincere Christian conscience and displaying a caring paternalism towards his workers. Over the years he bought more and more pockets of land to build housing on. Small bits of Port Sunlight seem to have escaped to other parts of the surrounding landscape and make it clear that his greatest vision was to have effectively turned the entire Wirral peninsula into one giant Garden City-type development. Sadly, following the death of his wife Lever lost interest in his more ambitious schemes, built the gallery as a memorial to her, but didn't complete his great housing experiment.

## Bournville

Bournville, on the outskirts of Birmingham, and sharing many of the characteristics of Port Sunlight,

An interesting variation in Bournville's generally well-behaved Arts and Crafts housing is this Voysey-esque house which apes all his mannerisms – battered buttresses, roughcast, and even the thin gutter brackets to the wide-boarded eaves.

was begun in 1893. Predominantly the work of only one architect, William Alexander Harvey, this is perhaps its most important difference from Port Sunlight and provides a consistency of architectural treatment. Here is a stripped-down version of Port Sunlight architecturally, perhaps more appropriate as its patrons were Quakers, less fanciful than Lever but every bit as socially committed. William Alexander Harvey was only twenty-one when appointed to design the houses for Bournville and they soon began to be noticed by influential magazines. In 1902 *The Studio* wrote that he had 'introduced a large variety into his designs, which are very quaint and picturesque and revive the best traditions of country architecture'.[126]

The idea of George Cadbury, who, together with his brother Richard took over the family's coffee and cocoa business from their father, it was at Bournville that artistry met economy. Although as philanthropic as Lever, the Cadburys built Bournville not merely for the employees of their new factory but for anyone who could afford the rents or sale price. If Bournville was a showpiece, it was to show how what was being called 'the cheap cottage problem' could be solved. By using standard elements, eliminating front rooms and long dark rear projections, and planning internal accommodation efficiently,

Harvey demonstrated an approach that soon made him an expert on the topic. Externally the houses are a mixture of exposed brick, rough pebbledash, and timber-framed vernacular details. Aiming at simplicity Harvey was clearly enthralled by contemporary architects such as Baillie Scott and Voysey and many of the houses echo some of their work at its best. On Mary Vale Road for example, we find Voysey's love of tall, battered buttresses, in turn mirrored in the shape of the chimney stack and even the joinery to the porch. Elsewhere dormers cut through eaves whilst the gutters, supported on slender etiolated metal brackets, continue the eaves line to maintain artistic balance (and cost) in the composition. Half-timbering, either false and for effect, or structural (as with Baillie Scott), is employed to suggest a manor house whereas we are looking at a series of four terraced houses. Elsewhere his houses resemble nothing so much as variations on Webb's Red House brought down the social scale to be more affordable.

Although he left Cadbury's employment to set up his own practice in 1904, Harvey stayed on at Bournville as a consultant and in 1906 published a summary of his work as 'The model village and its cottages; Bournville', to cement his expertise in the area of low-cost housing. But life at Bournville was not for everyone. Like Lever, the owning family were tee-total so there were no public houses and drunkenness was frowned upon. Additionally, gardens were expected to be maintained spotlessly or fines were imposed. Despite its appearance of freedom, as 'communities without conflict' (as the Italian historian Manfredo Tafuri has memorably called them) these were paternalistic undertakings by their industrialist owners. If you were happy to live in this way, effectively a medieval feudalistic lifestyle, then it provided a healthy, affordable and happy existence. If not, you had to find another job and leave.

## New Earswick

New Earswick, on the outskirts of York, was yet another model village for a chocolate manufacturer

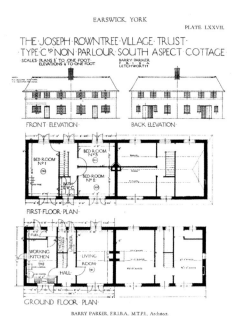

EARSWICK, YORK

PLATE LXXVII.

THE·JOSEPH·ROWNTREE·VILLAGE·TRUST·
·TYPE·C 1° NON·PARLOUR·SOUTH·ASPECT·COTTAGE·

FRONT·ELEVATION·  BACK·ELEVATION·

FIRST·FLOOR·PLAN·

GROUND·FLOOR·PLAN·

BARRY·PARKER, F.R.I.B.A., M.T.P.I., Architect.

Barry Parker's design for workers' housing at New Earswick eliminated the parlour, or 'room for best'. (James and Yerbury, *Small Houses for the Community*, 1924)

*and Common-sense* (1902). Here they argued for the complete abolition of 'backs, and back yards, back alleys and other such abominations . . .'[127] Designing working-class housing was a new area of work for architects and a specialization they sought to make their own in the light of the 'Profession or Art' debate of the 1880s and attempts to counter the threat of the general builder.

At New Earswick between 1902 and 1904, they only designed twenty-eight houses but they provide a clear indication of where garden city housing was headed. More utilitarian in appearance than Port Sunlight, or Bournville, New Earswick was informed by the book that set out the theory of the garden city and the organization that helped establish it as a reality. The book was called *Tomorrow; A Peaceful Path Toward Real Reform* (1898); the organization was the Garden City Association (1899).

## The utopian craft communities

(chocolate, and especially cocoa, being an essential weapon in the Temperance Movement) but closest both in design, and intention, to the idea of the Garden City Movement. It was created by Joseph Rowntree, who saw himself in competition with George Cadbury at Bournville and sought to provide decent housing for his workers. Where Port Sunlight employed thirty architects and Bournville just two, New Earswick sees the entrance onto the stage of Raymond Unwin and Barry Parker. Together this practice was more responsible than any other for the character and appearance of the Garden City. Vaguely related to each other, Unwin was a presence in Manchester in the 1880s as Secretary of the local Socialist League and a key member of the Northern Art Workers' Guild. Their relationship was cemented in 1893 when Unwin married Parker's sister Ethel and in 1896 the two men set up a practice in Buxton, specializing in working-class housing. This interest manifested itself not only in their architectural work but their influential publications such as *The Art of Building a Home* (1901) and *Cottage Plans*

For those who didn't live in cities the life of the rural poor, despite its challenges, was still largely unchanged and represented the ideals and way of life that Morris and his followers admired. And of course, it was this life which its more radical practitioners – people like Gimson and Ashbee – sought to live no less than Morris had hoped when he built the Red House as both his 'palace of art' and brotherhood of artists living a communal life. Ashbee brought 150 workmen of his Guild of Handicraft and their families from London's Whitechapel to Chipping Campden in 1901, arguing that 'we cannot do without country air'. The move to a beautiful unspoilt Cotswold market town was a bold undertaking and initially achieved some success. As he later wrote, 'We felt long before the move was made that to do our work of Arts and Crafts well we must get out into the country'. At Sapperton, Gimson and the Barnsley brothers established an ideal Arts and Crafts community when Lord Bathurst, the landowner, allowed them to build a series of cottages for

Around the turn of the century both private and public housing started to embrace the idea of living in flats. Here we see two blocks designed by the Collins family in Muswell Hill (Birchwood Mansions and The Gables) and some of the earliest council flats, Ruskin House, by the London County Council in Pimlico. Herbert Collins went on to design much Arts and Crafts-influenced housing in Southampton.

themselves – Beechanger, The Leasowes, and Upper Dorval House, whilst also leasing Daneway House as a showroom. Norman Jewson, writing of his time working for Gimson, recalled that, 'In his Utopia the greater part of the population would live in villages, each largely self-supporting with their farms, mills, wheelwrights, carpenters, masons and other tradesmen. There would be small towns producing goods beyond the capacity of the villages, and forms of culture and entertainment for their immediate districts, whilst a few larger towns would be centres of government, research, specialization, and so on.'[128]

It seems only the outbreak of the First World War stopped Gimson creating a craft village a few miles from Sapperton. He'd already bought the land, and

ensured a water supply, and was seeking financial backing from Ernest Debenham, the department store heir, shortly before his death in 1919. Debenham was a significant Arts and Crafts client who had employed Halsey Ricardo to design not only his own house – the shimmering Peacock House – in London in 1905 but, with MacDonald Gill, a small estate of forty agricultural workers' cottages at Briantspuddle in Dorset. Begun in 1914 and completed after the war it included experimental use of hollow concrete blocks for thatched cottages as a means of addressing the 'cheap cottage' problem.

It would be simplistic to suggest that these isolated utopian experiments and aspirations for communal living were much of an influence on the Garden City

Movement but there are clearly links between these small-scale idealistic craft communities and the fully realized dreams of the garden city pioneers. It's surely clear that in so many ways the Arts and Crafts Movement was haunted by the idea of the rural cottage and a simple village life.

## The theory of the garden city – Ebenezer Howard

The garden city really begins with the writings of Ebenezer Howard. Emerging out of the political debates of the 1880s and 1890s, in 1898 he published a seminal book entitled *Tomorrow: A Peaceful Path Towards Reform*. It is an interesting title and well worth mulling over for what it tells the reader about the thinking behind it. That isolated single word title – 'Tomorrow' – immediately identifies it as being in the tradition of utopian fiction. Other works such as Edward Bellamy's *Looking Backwards*, based on Thomas Moore's *Utopia* (and perhaps ultimately Plato's *Republic*) were its ancestors. Indeed much of Morris's work, such as *News from Nowhere* and *A Dream of John Bull* was also in this well-established literary genre of imaginative wish-fulfilment. But why 'peaceful'? Here we return to the fears of revolution that partly informed the Great Exhibition in 1851. Although an uprising never materialized, a 'peaceful path' was very much wanted – even the idea of a path, rather than a road, evokes Howard's gentle rural vision of progressive politics. If it could be accomplished, reform, rather than revolution, would be the result of Howard's work and all achieved through the establishment of garden cities.

It's important to stress that Howard was not an architect, nor a member of the Arts and Crafts Movement, but a parliamentary reporter who, in common with many of his generation, was attracted to politics via radical progressive organizations such as the Fabians, Quakers and the Christian Socialists. His book gives the abstract theoretical principles of what garden cities should be and how they could work economically and socially. In the plans drawn in the book

he is careful to make it clear that his ideas are only guidelines and the actual site conditions should dictate the layout of the new settlements. It relied upon others to implement his ideas, give them physical form, and create the architecture and layout of the garden city. Despite this qualification he clearly had a strong vision of the new towns, seeing them as combining the best of the town and the best of the countryside – what he called the 'town and country magnet' – to form this new type of development, the garden city.

His prescription for these utopian new settlements was quite clear. A group of wealthy philanthropic individuals form a co-partnership company and the company buy 6,000 acres of cheap agricultural land away from existing centres of population but close enough to feed off a central city of 58,000. The appalling housing conditions of Victorian England had already led many such philanthropists to invest in better housing for a modest financial return of only five per cent, earning themselves the ironic title of 'five per cent philanthropists'. Profits from the company would be largely ploughed, almost literally, back into the garden city with the investors content to make a very small profit. All residents were to be shareholders, giving them a say over how the city was run as a form of co-operative living. Just as Ruskin

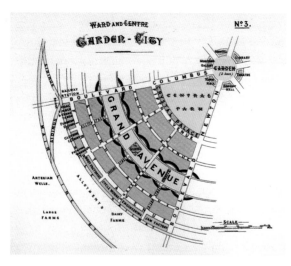

A diagram from Howard's book explains the principle of zoning the garden city.

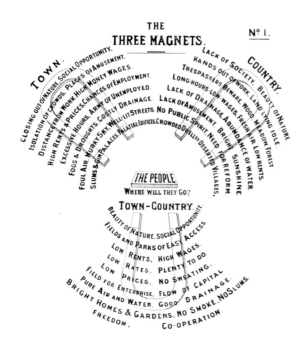

THE
THREE MAGNETS.                    Nº 1.

A graphic portrayal of Howard's idea of the 'Town and Country magnet' combining the best of both worlds to create garden cities.

therefore of the shares, would also increase to make it a commercial success. Then as the town reached its population limits this would allow a new 6,000 acres of cheap agricultural land to be bought in another part of the country and the whole 'experiment' repeated, with the result that a series of garden city satellites were built, all related to the central city. Eventually the country could be covered with small, independent, self-sufficient, financially successful towns and cities built according to progressive political ideas and giving their inhabitants a better, healthier way of life. Utopian indeed. But how was this theory to become reality?

## Theory into practice: early developments

In 1899, the year after publication of Howard's book, the Garden City Association was founded to promote Howard's ideas through the establishment of the first garden city. Although the credit for establishing the essential co-partnership principles of Howard's theory is normally given to Letchworth, begun in 1903, it was Brentham in the London suburb of Ealing which first saw his economic theory put into practice.

Built in three main phases between 1901 and 1915, the Brentham Garden Suburb was a development of just 680 houses and flats. The initial phase was designed by the architect Frederick Pearson and at first sight the housing seems anything but Arts and Crafts, despite his delight in vernacular detail, varied roof outlines, and picturesque site planning – possibly already following the latest Arts and Crafts ideas – marking it out as distinctive. The company that established the estate, the Ealing Tenants Ltd, initially commissioned Pearson to design around 100 terraced houses. These were built between 1901 and 1906, but in a typically Edwardian style. In 1907 the look of the estate was to change considerably with the appointment of Raymond Unwin as the company's architect. In 1911 a third architect, George Sutcliffe (later involved in a large number of garden city-type housing developments), was appointed to succeed

had argued for the freedom inherent in craftsmen to be of importance, so the same freedoms were now being given to residents of the garden city.

To establish a garden city, Howard proposed that of the 6,000 acres bought, only 1,000 were to be built on. The rest was to be given over to agriculture with the aim that the new settlement becomes self-sufficient, together with ample public parks and individual gardens attached to houses to improve the quality of life. The outer edge of the land was to be left undeveloped to form 'a green belt' to physically restrict the kind of unregulated expansion that had created such vast slums as existed on the edges of many large Victorian towns – the 'monstrosities of haphazard growth' that Morris condemned. Civic and communal buildings were to be provided in the centre of the city, industry and agriculture to the edge, and low-density good-quality housing in-between. Just as the green belt restricted expansion physically, so too the population of the new towns and cities was to be limited to 32,000 people. Howard's theory was that as the prosperity of the garden city grew so the value of the land, and

A row of houses in Brentham uses render, dormers, projections and set-backs to vary the profile from the typical nineteenth-century terrace – and all are placed in generous gardens.

Unwin and adopted an altogether more utilitarian set of design principles. Brentham's significance is to have been the first development to follow the co-partnership principles outlined by Howard. Historically significant though this is, it fell to Parker and Unwin to clothe the estate in the aesthetic ideas of the Arts and Crafts Movement they had already employed at New Earswick, and went on to expand at Letchworth.

## Letchworth Garden City – the dream realized

Begun in 1903, Letchworth was built by 'First Garden City Ltd', the first housing (appropriately called Alpha Cottages) being completed in 1904. A limited competition was held for the overall plan to demonstrate how Howard's theory could be realized on the ground and three practices were invited to enter. These were Geoffrey Lucas and Sidney Cranfield, W.R. Lethaby and Halsey Ricardo, and Barry Parker and Raymond Unwin. The latter won with a design that took account of the existing topography of the area (only one tree was felled during construction) and laid out a formal city centre with radiating avenues and cottage-style housing on informal irregular lanes. At this time Parker and Unwin's approach was being greatly influenced by the contemporary Austrian architect and planner Camillo Sitte. In 1889 he had published a

work entitled *City Planning According to Artistic Principles* which, as the title suggested, looked at the new science of planning cities as an artistic activity as much as a practical one. By analysing examples of what he saw as artistically successful towns in northern Europe, he came up with the principle of creating 'street pictures'. Various techniques to create such pictures were adopted so that, for example, vistas were terminated by buildings, or the curve of the road cut the view off rather than stretching on endlessly into infinity. Important lessons that Parker and Unwin took from Sitte were that straight lines, as found in bye-law housing, were an anathema, so breaking up a terrace became important, as did limiting its length. This could be done by laying out smaller terraces in a staggered, seemingly random line informally, or even simply having sections of the terrace project forward and back to create more interest and variety of outline.

In contrast, Lethaby and Ricardo's competition entry suggests a more formal, almost military, arrangement of blocks of housing arranged neatly around the edge of their plots, allowing daylight into the gardens hidden behind but like a small series of domestic barracks backing onto a parade ground. This is most likely the Lethaby of 'Town Tidying', a lecture he gave to the Art Workers' Guild in 1916 that included '. . . an example of what I mean by art where order, construction, beauty, and efficiency are all one, may I instance the Navy?'[129]

The sheer size of Letchworth was ambitious and as it grew, it attracted large numbers of visitors. Many came to view the 'Cheap Cottages exhibitions' held in 1905 and 1907. Here architects demonstrated innovative new ideas in the planning and construction of housing such as prefabrication and the use of concrete, techniques and materials generally opposed by many Arts and Crafts architects. But then the houses had to be capable of being built for £150 – the cost having been calculated that would allow affordable rents to be charged. The actual cost, taking into account architects' fees and builders' costs, was more like £250. A further tension was that the competition

Rushby Way in Letchworth Garden City. Designed by Barry Parker and Raymond Unwin, who also planned the entire new city and put the clothes on Howard's radical ideas.

The Mrs Howard Memorial Hall in Letchworth. Opened in 1905, it was the city's first public building and quickly became a centre for literary, musical and political life.

was also part of the attempt to get around the high standards of construction now demanded by law. Building on private land not regulated by a local council meant the use of expensive materials such as brick and stone wasn't necessary, but buildings still had to be approved by Parker and Unwin as architects to the First Garden City Ltd. Amongst the winners of the first competition was Percy Houfton, who had been designing improved workers' housing for the Bolsover and Cresswell Colliery Company in Derbyshire. Lord Northcliffe, the proprietor of the *Daily Mail*, sponsored the exhibition but was opposed to the creation of the architectural profession because of its charges, not its artistic credentials, and the 'Cheap Cottages exhibition' eventually led in 1908 to the newspaper establishing the *Ideal Home* exhibitions.

Parker, Unwin and Howard all moved to Letchworth as work commenced, with Unwin designing a large asymmetrical semi-detached house in Letchworth Lane, clearly borrowing much from earlier designs for New Earswick. Elsewhere good examples of stripped-down Arts and Crafts houses abound, such as 102 Wilbury Road (1908–09), a deceptive three-storey house for Parker's brother Stanley, which is more roof than wall to convey safety and security – as well as reducing building costs. A large gable end displays the three storeys, but all is red tile and white render – the large over-sailing roof seeming to be staked to the

This modest house by Percy Houfton, an architect with a reputation for housing for miners, was one of the winners in the 'Cheap Cottages' exhibition of 1905, which resulted in 130 houses of varying design being built. Unusually one of the entries was designed by a woman, Elspeth McClelland, nicknamed 'the Suffragette architect'. The exhibition attracted over 60,000 visitors.

ground by its solid square chimney stack lest it blow away. Housing groups on Birds Hill (1907) by Parker and Unwin, and Rushby Mead (1911–12) by Bennett and Bidwell, and Courtenay Crickmer, for example

It's hard to believe this cottage, designed by Baillie Scott, hasn't stood in Letchworth for hundreds of years.

contain short terraces of four cottages designed as single compositions, their ends terminated by projecting gable blocks, walls by simple bay windows, roofs punctured by varied dormers, and laid out to follow the irregular pattern of the street. The careful design of such blocks recalls the traditional architecture of the Cotswolds and went on to set models for the 'Homes fit for Heroes' council housing programme after the First World War. The other established names who designed for Letchworth included Baillie Scott, whose Elmwood and Tanglewood of 1907 are quintessential Arts and Crafts houses, sparse on decoration, loving in detail, and unified in white render.

## The influence of the garden city experiment

The success of Letchworth led to many imitators. In 1909 Lutyens wrote to his friend Herbert Baker that, 'There is a boom coming for Garden Cities', and he was right.[130] Many of these were merely replicating the informal layout and cottage-type architecture that characterized them but were private estates built for profit. In itself this was a demonstration of the enormous appeal of the garden city aesthetic but not its social conscience. These places effectively hijacked the vision of the garden city and used it for profit, creating

an illusion of financial and political freedom that did not exist. One of the most attractive of these has to be the houses in and around The Close at Llanfairfechan in North Wales, designed by Herbert North with the architect acting as the developer also. Trained under Sedding and Lutyens, North's white-rendered houses take every advantage the mountainous landscape of North Wales has to offer. Others were more politically motivated and were established as proper co-partnership schemes such as Fallings Park, Wolverhampton, begun in 1907. Here an estate of 4,000 homes was planned – including designs by Randall Wells – but less than eighty houses were built before the war halted development. Further north Oldham Garden Suburb, begun in 1909 by Mary Higgs, the leader of the 'Beautiful Oldham Society', and an early member of the Garden Cities Association, came into being following a visit to Parker and Unwin's Hampstead Garden Suburb. Of the 700 planned houses only eighty-three were built before the war. Other developments such as Wavertree (known at the time as the Liverpool Garden Suburb and with housing designed by George Sutcliffe, who had worked on Brentham) and Rhiwbina Garden Village near Cardiff (by Parker and Unwin) met similar fates and were only partially realized before the war. Some, such as Sheffield's Flower estate, or Romford's Gidea Park, began as a form of 'Cheap Cottage' exhibition similar to that held in Letchworth. The Flower estate at High

Herbert North's houses straddle the edge of Snowdonia at Llanfairfechan.

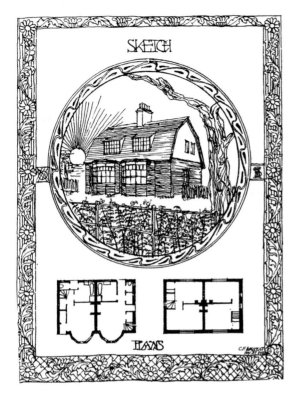

C.F. Innocent's florid drawing to accompany his entry for the Yorkshire and North Midlands Model Cottage Exhibition in Sheffield, 1907. A private development undertaken in response to Letchworth's 1905 'Cheap Cottage' exhibition, the Corporation subsequently acquired all the houses.

Wincobank began following the Corporation's acquisition of the land in 1900. The competition houses were built between 1903–04 to a layout by Alexander Harvey of Bournville, now specializing in garden city-type housing developments with his new partner A. McKewan. The competition for workmen's houses was again won by Percy Houfton on the back of his experience designing improved colliery housing in the Derbyshire coalfields.

Time and again the same names crop up involved with these disparate settlements across the country, a testament to the widespread influence of the Garden City Association and the network of architects employed. At Romford these included not only Parker and Unwin, but also Ashbee, Baillie Scott, Houfton, Williams-Ellis, Jewson and Green. Perhaps more importantly the judges of the competition were largely composed of members of the Arts and Crafts

Movement, including Ernest Gimson, Halsey Ricardo, Walter Cave, Guy Dawber and Mervyn Macartney.

## The impact of the First World War

It might be reasonably assumed that with the outbreak of the First World War in 1914, housing reform would take a back seat and give way to the demands of a war-time economy where speed and quantity would have to take precedence over craftsmanship and quality. In many respects this is true, with large camps of temporary housing created up and down the country to support the war effort. However, in a remarkable series of developments the war was arguably the greatest success of the garden city approach and enabled it to become the dominant approach to state housing between the wars. The opportunity came about because of the political scandal of the so-called 'shell crisis', which saw the British artillery running out of shells in the early stages of the war. To increase production new factories were quickly built, and the architects in the government's Office of Works were instructed to design new housing estates for the increase in munitions workers. So enormous was the problem a new Ministry of Munitions, led by Lloyd George, was created in 1915 and Raymond Unwin made its chief architect. By this date Unwin had published *Town Planning in Practice; An Introduction to the Art of Designing Cities and Suburbs* (1909) which, using examples from Letchworth and elsewhere, had quickly become the standard book on the subject. In 1910 the RIBA held the world's first International Conference on Town Planning in London and confirmed the country's dominance in this new field.

Once in post, Unwin had the example of the housing built by the Office of Works under one of its principal architects, Frank Baines, before him. At Well Hall, and soon after at Roe Green, Baines (who had worked in Ashbee's office) employed garden city layouts, densities and housing standards despite the pressure to build quickly and cheaply. Working with a talented team of young architects, estates such as

Frank Baines, in his role as Principal Architect to the Office of Works, designed this estate at Roe Green for workers in the nearby Aircraft Manufacturing Company factory as part of the government's push to maintain armament production in the First World War. The estate's variety came both from his design principles and the scarcity of materials at any one time. It was built using fast-track American systems of manufacture.

## 'Homes fit for Heroes' and post-war council housing

The standards set in munitions housing were so impressive that once thoughts turned to solving the housing problems at the end of the war the work of Baines, Unwin, and other official architects who were formed by the values of the Arts and Crafts Movement naturally led the way and their ideas brought together in the influential Tudor Walters Report of 1919. The recommendations here soon became official government housing policy to the extent that it formed the basis of the 1919 Housing Act and more importantly its associated housing manual. Known as the Addison Act, it was the culmination of the 'Homes fit for Heroes' campaign, which ably argued that better quality housing should be seen as a reward for the sacrifice made during the war – 'Nothing gained by overcrowding', as the title of a pamphlet by Unwin argued in 1912. It was also quite clear that if housing standards didn't improve after the war the returning troops were likely to take matters into their own hands and revolution, as had happened in Russia in 1917, was a possible consequence. As such the Housing Act was a counter-revolutionary measure. It allowed the lives of men and women shattered by the trauma of their war-time experience to recover in the nostalgic and almost therapeutic embrace of these garden-city landscapes they had fought for. A pioneering piece of legislation, it created over 1.3 million homes and provided the framework for council housing for the next forty years. Here at last, with the financial support of the government (not merely a handful of philanthropic individuals), was the key to providing Arts and Crafts for all in the form of state-subsidized housing that all could afford.

Despite its ubiquity and seeming lack of individuality there could be considerable regional variation in these 'Homes fit for Heroes'. In a way that echoed both the variety of housing created by material shortages at Well Hall, but also the respect for local building traditions so strongly felt

Well Hall (serving the expanded Royal Arsenal at Woolwich) and Roe Green (serving the local aircraft factories of A.V. Roe) exemplified the principles established at Letchworth and elsewhere. If anything they were visually more successful than their predecessors due to the variety of external treatment caused by the war-time shortages of materials. Some have timber cladding to the upper floors or just gable ends, others have hung tiles, slates, or even shingles, others still simple roughcast render, a few merely bare brick but laid with delight in its decorative possibilities. The overall effect is a closer approximation to Charles Wade's drawings of the imaginary village in *Town Planning in Practice* than anything previously built. As a local newspaper reported early in 1916 during a visit to Well Hall by Lever and Cadbury, 'When sun and wind and rain have had their will with its fresh tints, and its newness has had time to mellow, Well Hall will look like nothing in the world so much as an old characteristic village of the English countryside – as full of lines and curves as a lane or a hedge, as full of colour as a bean field.'[131] By the end of the war the Ministry of Munitions had built thirty-eight new housing estates for its 300 new factories.

The roads and pavements are still not made up and children play happily in the sun in this contemporary photograph of a new 'Homes fit for Heroes' estate in Dover. (James and Yerbury, *Small Houses for the Community*, 1924)

by the likes of Webb and his followers, local housing authorities kept costs down by using local materials. Hence a council house in one district could, and often did, look very different in another. One of the most striking examples of this is provided by a row of semi-detached council houses built in 1922 in Ponsanooth, Cornwall. Designed by P. Edwin Stevens, they are built of granite, with hipped roofs covered in local slate sweeping down to the porch and fit perfectly into the local landscape. In other parts of the country, such as rural Kent, clay tile hanging, catslide roofs, and other vernacular details drawn from local examples take precedence.

The London County Council's Architects Department, through its Housing of the Working Classes branch, had been quick to establish 'cottage estates' before the war and now expanded their council housing programme enormously with eight new estates built between 1919 and 1929 on the outskirts of London. The Watling estate at Burnt Oak, built between 1924 and 1927, employs the local Home Counties vernacular of timber cladding to supply variety. Many estates were vast. The Downham estate, the third largest, was constructed between 1924 and 1930 and provided 7,000 new homes for a population of 29,000. Elsewhere, following the donation of land by Ernst Simon, Manchester Corporation employed Barry Parker to lay out and design the Wythenshawe

estate in 1927, which on completion was the largest in Europe. At their height such developments were the envy of the world and continued to use pioneering new construction techniques and materials as the 'Cheap Cottages' exhibitions had done. Its architects, such as Archibald Soutar who worked on the Old Oak estate and whose brother, J.C. Soutar, had replaced Unwin at Hampstead Garden Suburb in 1914, had trained under the architects of the Arts and Crafts Movement.

The immediate post-war years saw council housing being built that reflected regional variation and used local materials – as this granite-built example (one of six) of 1922 by P. Edwin Stevens in Ponsanooth, Cornwall, so ably demonstrates, even down to the Cornish hedge garden wall. It was completed just as the financial subsidy that enabled it was withdrawn.

The Watling estate in north London is one of twelve cottage estates built by the London County Council after the war and designed along garden city lines. The estate grew to over 4,000 houses of varied design under the LCC's chief architect, George Topham Forrest, including these experimental wooden houses of which 400 were built in the hopes of being quicker and cheaper to build to meet the demand . . . and stave off fears of revolution! The estate was nicknamed 'Little Moscow'.

## Conclusion

Today the cottage estates of council housing built in reverence for the pre-industrial life admired by the Arts and Crafts Movement still provide homes across the length and breadth of the country. Were he alive today, Morris might need to reflect on his statement that, 'I spend my life in ministering to the swinish luxury of the rich.' His ultimate achievement was that his 'palace of art' – the Red House – led to the 'palaces for the people' of council housing. The Garden City Movement created enclaves of great beauty and retreat on the edge of our towns and cities, and a better way of life for the many it lifted out of the slums.

Still going strong, these council houses in West Sussex still display all the principles of the Garden City Movement.

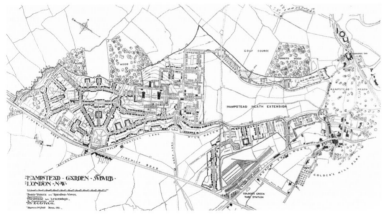

The definitive plan for the layout of Hampstead Garden Suburb as published in 1911, five years after building began. Notice the clear straight line in the middle where the Great Wall made the limits of the estate clear. (Raymond Unwin, *Town Planning in Practice*, 2nd ed., 1909)

without jobs the workers whose lives were to benefit from the better housing and living conditions would be unable to afford to live there. The idea of a garden suburb was that it allowed its residents to work elsewhere and commute back and forth between work and decent living conditions. In the case of Hampstead these commuter journeys were enabled by the introduction of cheap workmen's fares on the trains from nearby Golders Green and Highgate stations. Yet its genesis was not simply a concern to help the least well off but an early environmental campaign to save valuable open land on the edge of London.

In 1906, with help from a long list of notable subscribers, 243 acres were bought by a company established as the Hampstead Garden Suburb Trust Ltd., to be run as a co-partnership scheme. It was the brainchild of Henrietta Barnett who, together with her husband the Canon Samuel Barnett, had helped the poor of the East End of London not only by the establishment of the Whitechapel Art Gallery, but more importantly Toynbee Hall, one of the first university settlements, and the one out of which Ashbee's Guild of Handicrafts had been born earlier. Henrietta Barnett, aware of the work at Letchworth,

As a final case study, the creation of Hampstead Garden Suburb neatly sums up many important aspects of Arts and Crafts architecture as a whole. Hampstead Garden Suburb was clearly not, as its name suggests, a garden city, but a suburb of London laid out on parts of

Hampstead Heath. Implicit in both its creation, and its name, was the recognition that garden cities such as Letchworth would take a long time to become economically successful and achieve the self-sufficiency that was dreamed of. The attempts to bring industry to Letchworth were difficult and

Arcade House (1914) at Temple Fortune by A.J. Penty – one of two such blocks of shops with flats above, they act as a form of ceremonial entrance and 'city wall' to the suburb beyond.

A classic garden city-type block of houses in Asmun's Place (1907–08) treated as a unified composition. This is one of the suburb's earliest at the crown of a cul-de-sac – a device created at Hampstead Garden Suburb – in the Artisan's Quarter.

One of the squares on Corringham Road (1911–12) by Parker and Unwin show them moving from Arts and Crafts informality to the orderliness of a more Classical or Georgian design. The repetition is broken by the brick and stone chequerboard pattern over the central door.

employed Parker and Unwin to lay out a housing estate on a small part of the heath in order to save the greater part as open land for all. They created very clearly demarked boundaries, so to the high ground off Temple Fortune Lane, blocks of flats by A.J. Penty are designed like some Bavarian medieval hill-top town. These dominant corner blocks with open arcades, flats above and shops below, create nothing so much as giant gateways into this Arts and Crafts arcadia. To the south a more intimate and rural tone is created by the great

boundary wall designed by Charles Wade, peppered with attractive garden gazebos like watch towers, from which to admire the views of the heath.

Between these boundaries Parker and Unwin employed the same principles they had used at Letchworth derived from both Sitte's ideas and the romance of English vernacular architecture. Being governed by the existing legislation, the Trust had to secure

an Act of Parliament in 1906 to be allowed to build houses to the low densities needed, and particularly for the introduction of that most quintessentially suburban road layout, the cul-de-sac. The cul-de-sac maximized the number of houses that could be grouped around the drains, thus reducing the overall cost. However, as the roads were short and went nowhere they could, if the law allowed, be built to a lower standard to save costs. Aesthetically

Gazebos, like modest look-out towers, stretch along the so-called 'Great Wall' with doors like sally-ports to let residents onto Hampstead Heath. Designed (and drawn) by C.P. Wade, it's a statement of principle – we will build no further. In the background are varied housing clusters around St Jude's Church designed by Edwin Lutyens in the communal heart of the suburb. (Raymond Unwin, *Town Planning in Practice*, 2nd ed., 1909)

Geoffrey Lucas designed this varied group of twelve houses off Hampstead Way around a communal sunken tennis court. The drawing was exhibited at the Royal Academy in 1909. (*Academy Architecture*, 1909) See also overleaf.

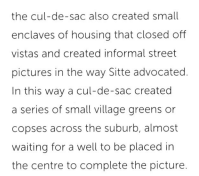

the cul-de-sac also created small enclaves of housing that closed off vistas and created informal street pictures in the way Sitte advocated. In this way a cul-de-sac created a series of small village greens or copses across the suburb, almost waiting for a well to be placed in the centre to complete the picture.

As a suburb there was no need for a civic centre as had to be created at Letchworth and other later garden cities. However, to be just a random development of attractive well-designed housing would merely add to urban sprawl, as some of the vast London council estates did, and was not

sufficient for Barnett and her sponsors. Accordingly Howard's ideas were still followed, so the suburb included at its centre two churches and an institute set amongst gardens on one of the heath's highest points. Designed by Lutyens in a quasi-Classical idiom – part Neo-Georgian, part Wrenaissance, part Byzantine – these monumental public buildings were the perfect foil to the vernacular-style houses by Parker and Unwin and a host of others which then spread out along the suburb's meandering curvaceous roads, cul-de-sacs, and lawns. One of the more interesting buildings was Waterlow Court designed by Baillie Scott for Sir Sidney Waterlow's Industrial Dwellings Company in 1909. The court – part alms house, part cloister, part quad, and part private square – was built specifically for unmarried working

women as a series of three- to five-roomed flats. To the ground floor, an open arcade of semi-circular arches creates the feeling of enclosure and safety whilst the composition is grounded by a large communal dining hall.

So influential was the suburb, and especially being easier to visit than Letchworth, that early cottage estates by the London County Council paid homage to it in developments such as the Old Oak estate, Hammersmith, begun in 1912 and what has been called 'the culminating achievement of the Council's venture into garden suburb planning before the first world war'.[132] Today Hampstead Garden Suburb contains the largest and best collection of Arts and Crafts housing to be found anywhere in the country.

1. William Morris, 'The Decorative Arts: Their Relation to Modern Life and Progress'. This was Morris's first public lecture, later published as 'The Lesser Arts' in *Hopes and Fears for Art* (London, Ellis & White, 1882).

2. The SPAB manifesto can be viewed at https://www.spab.org.uk/about-us/spab- manifesto (accessed 20.3.19).

3. E.T. Cook & A. Wedderburn, *The Complete Works of John Ruskin* (London, Allen & Unwin, 1903–12) vol. 10, p.192.

4. E.S. Prior, 'Texture as a quality of art and a condition for architecture', *Transactions of the National Association for the Advancement of Art and its Application to Industry* (London, NAAAAI, 1890) p.326.

5. Reginald Blomfield, *Studies in Architecture* (London, 1905) p.1.

6. Charles Voysey, '1874 and After', *Architectural Review* (vol. 70, 1931) pp.91–2.

7. Lawrence Weaver, *Small Country Houses of To-day* (London, Country Life, [second series] 1919) p.20.

8. John Betjeman, 'Mackay Hugh Baillie Scott', *The Journal of the Manx Museum* (vol. VII, no.84, 1968).

9. Mackay Hugh Baillie Scott, 'The Cheap Cottage', *The Studio* (vol. 61, 1914) p.135.

10. J.D. Sedding, 'The Handicrafts in Old Days', *Art and Handicraft* (London, K. Paul, Trench, Trübner, 1893) p.63.

11. Norman Jewson, *By Chance I Did Rove* (Barnsley, Gryffon Publications, 1986) p.16.

12. Cook *op. cit.*

13. H.S. Goodhart-Rendel, 'Architectural Memoirs', *The Architectural Review* (January 1957) pp.147–8.

14. May Morris, *RIBA Journal*, 20 February 1932, p.303.

15. W.R. Lethaby, *Philip Webb and his Work* (Oxford, Oxford University Press, 1935) pp.94–5.

16. Betjeman, *op. cit.*

17. William Morris, *op. cit.*

18. Arts and Crafts Exhibition Society, *Arts and Crafts Essays by Members of the Arts and Crafts Exhibition Society* (London, Green and Co., 1893) p.412.

19. R. Norman Shaw and T.G. Jackson (eds.), *Architecture; A Profession or an Art* (London, John Murray, 1892) p.vii.

20. *Ibid*, p.168.

21. Edgar Wood, 'From Nature to Design', *Northern Art Workers' Guild; Catalogue of Works Exhibited by Members* (Manchester, Chorlton & Knowles, 1898) p.10.

22. R. Randal Phillips, *The Modern English House* (London, Country Life, 1920) p.ix.

23. *The British Architect* (vol. 35, April 17, 1891) p.290.

24. W.R. Lethaby, *Architecture* (London, Williams & Norgate, 1911) p.249.

25. Robert Macleod, *Style and Society; Architectural Ideology in Britain 1835–1914* (London, RIBA, 1971) p.67.

26. Reginald Blomfield, *The Mistress Art* (London, Edward Arnold, 1908) p.99.

27. Quoted in Michael W. Brooks, *John Ruskin and Victorian Architecture* (London, Thames & Hudson, 1989) p.124.

28. Cook, *op. cit.*, vol. 12, p.419.

29. *Ibid*, p.624.

30. R. Daniels & G. Brandwood (eds.), *Ruskin and Architecture* (Reading, Spire Books Ltd., 2003) p.81.

31. Benjamin Ferry, *Recollections of A.N. Welby Pugin, and his Father, Augustus Pugin; With Notices of their Works.* (London, E. Stanford, 1861) p.45.

32. Rosemary Hill, *God's Archtect; Pugin and the Building of Romantic Britain* (London, Allen Lane, 2007), p.359.

33. A.W.N. Pugin, *The True Principles of Pointed or Christian Architecture* (London, J. Weale, 1841) p.14.

34. Hermann Muthesius, *The English House*, (London, Crosby Lockwood Staples, 1979) p.13 [abridged translation of three volumes of *Das Englische Haus* of 1908–11].

35. E.T. Cook, *The Life of John Ruskin, volume 1.* (London, Allen & Unwin, 1911) p.449.

36. J.W. Mackail, *The Life of William Morris* (London, Longmans Green & Co., 1901) vol. 1, p.113.

37. Lethaby, *op. cit.*, p.122.

38. P. Thompson, *The Work of William Morris* (London, Quartet, 1977) p.83.

39. N. Kelvin (ed.), *The Collected Letters of William Morris* (Princeton, Princeton University Press, 1984) pp.185–6. Morris to Scheu, letter of 5 September 1883.

40. Mackail, *op. cit.*, p.147.

41. W.E. Fredeman (ed.), *The Correspondence of Dante Gabriel Rossetti*, (Woodbridge, D.S. Brewer, 2004) pp.62–3.

42. Mackail, *op. cit.*, p.160.

43. Cook & Wedderburn, *op. cit.* (vol. 10) p.245.

44. *Ibid.*

45. *Ibid.*, p.234.

46. Rory Spence et al, *A School of Rational Builders* (London, SPAB, 1982) p.22.

47. *Ibid.*, p.5.

48. Adrian Tinniswood, *The Arts and Crafts House* (London, Mitchell Beazley, 2005), p.24.

49. W.R. Lethaby et al, *Ernest Gimson; His Life and Work* (Stratford-upon-Avon, Shakespeare Head Press, 1924) p.4.

50. Kelvin, *op. cit.*, p.730.

51. Michael Hall, '"A Patriotism in our Art": Ideas of Englishness in the Architecture of G.F. Bodley', David Crellin and Ian Dungavell (eds.), *Architecture and Englishness, 1880–1914* (London, The Society of Architectural Historians of Great Britain, 2006) p.14.

52. Roderick Gradidge, *Dream Houses: The Edwardian Ideal* (London, Constable, 1980) p.66.

53. *Country Life* (11 June, 1910) p.846.

54. W.R. Lethaby, *Architecture, Mysticism, and Myth* (London, Percival & Co., 1892) p.8.

55. The National Trust, *Standen House and Garden* (Swindon, Acorn Press, 2007) p.37.
56. Reginald Blomfield, *Richard Norman Shaw R.A.* (London, 1940) p.98.
57. Brian Thomas, *Journal of the RIBA* (vol. lxiv, 1957) p.218.
58. Lethaby, *op. cit* (1892) p.xxiv.
59. W.R. Lethaby, 'Architectural Education; a discussion', *The Architectural Review* (vol. xvi, 1904) p.161.
60. B.G. Burrough, 'Three disciples of William Morris: 2. W.R. Lethaby', *Connoisseur*, 173, 1970.
61. Quoted in Godfrey Rubens' introduction to W.R. Lethaby, *Philip Webb and his Work* (London, Raven Oak Press, 1979 reprint of 1935 edition) p.iv.
62. Lethaby, *op. cit.* (1935) p.1.
63. Martin Cook, *Edward Prior: Arts and Crafts Architect* (Marlborough, Crowood Press, 2015), p.37.
64. Andrew Saint, *Richard Norman Shaw*, London, Yale University Press, 1976) p.186.
65. Cook, *op. cit.* (2015) p.420.
66. Prior, *op. cit.*
67. Walter Crane, *An Artist's Reminiscences* (London, Methuen, 1907) pp.324–5.
68. Muthesius, *op. cit.*, p.129.
69. Anon, *The Builder* (1895) p.323.
70. G. Hoare and G. Pyne, *Prior's Barn and Gimson's Coxen: Two Arts and Crafts Houses* (Budleigh Salterton, privately published, 1978), p.20.
71. *Country Life*, 6 November 1909, p.634.
72. *Ibid.*, p.636.
73. *Ibid.*, p.639.
74. Quoted in Cook, *op. cit.*, p.44.
75. Edward Prior, 'Correspondence, Roker Church', *The Builder* (23 November, 1907) p.563.
76. Nikolaus Pevsner, *The Buildings of England; Herefordshire* (Harmondsworth, Penguin, 1963), p.90.
77. Peter Blundell Jones, 'All Saints', Brockhampton', *The Architects' Journal* (15 August 1990) p.26.
78. G. Rubens, *W.R. Lethaby, His Life and Work 1857–1931* (London, The Architectural Press, 1986) p.154.
79. Jones, *op. cit.*, p.42.
80. Charles Voysey, *Individuality* (London, Chapman & Hall, 1915) p.1.
81. John Betjeman, 'Mackay Hugh Baillie Scott', *The Journal of the Manx Museum* (vol. VII, no. 84) 1968.
82. Sir Edwin Lutyens, Foreword to special issue devoted to Voysey, *Architectural Review* (vol.70, 1931) p.91.
83. Voysey, *op. cit.* (1931) p.92.
84. Muthesius, *op. cit.*, p.42.
85. Horace Townsend, interview with Charles Voysey, *The Studio* (vol. xvi, 1899) p.158.
86. Charles Voysey, 'The English Home', *The British Architect* (lxxv, 1911) p.70.
87. Wendy Hitchmough, *C.F.A.Voysey* (London, Phaidon, 1995) p.96.
88. M.H. Baillie Scott, 'On the Characteristics of Mr C.F.A. Voysey's Architecture', *The Studio* (42, October 1907) p.19.
89. Betjeman, *op. cit.*
90. *Ibid.*
91. M.H. Baillie Scott, *Houses and Gardens* (London, George Newnes, 1906) p.5.
92. Diane Haigh, Baillie Scott; *The Artistic House* (Chichester, John Wiley and Sons, 1995) p.56.
93. *Country Life*, 30 January 1904, p.162.
94. C. Percy and J. Ridley (eds.), *The Letters of Edwin Lutyens to his Wife Lady Emily Lutyens* (London, Collins, 1985) p.236.
95. A.S.G. Butler, *Domestic Architecture of Lutyens* (Woodbridge, Antique Collectors Club, 1989).
96. Betjeman, *op. cit.*
97. Peter Savage, *Lorimer and the Edinburgh Craft Designers* (London, Steve Savage publishers, 2005) p.25.
98. A. Stuart Gray, *Edwardian Architecture; A Biographical Dictionary* (London, Duckworth, 1985) p.243.
99. C. Percy, *op. cit.*, p.202.
100. H. Goodhart-Rendel, *Journal of the Royal Institute of British Architects* (1945) p.127.
101. Christopher Hussey, *The Life of Sir Edwin Lutyens* (London, Country Life, 1950) p.27.
102. Gavin Stamp, *Edwin Lutyens' Country Houses: From the Archives of Country Life* (London, Country Life, 2001) p.20.
103. *Ibid.*, p.66.
104. *Ibid.*, p.25.
105. John Brandon-Jones et al. 'Reminiscences of Sir Edwin Lutyens', *AA Journal* (lxxiv, March 1959) p.233.
106. Gradidge, *op. cit.*, p.191.
107. Ian MacDonald-Smith, *Arts and Crafts Master: The Houses and Gardens of M.H. Baillie Scott* (New York, Rizzoli, 2010) p.52.
108. C.F. Innocent, *The Development of English Building Construction* (Cambridge, Cambridge University Press,1916), p.3.
109. P.H. Ditchfield, *Vanishing England* (London, Methuen, 1910) p.2.
110. Michael Drury, *Wandering Architects: In Pursuit of an Arts and Crafts Ideal* (Stamford, Shaun Tyas Press, 2000).
111. Jewson, *op. cit.*, p.1.
112. Muthesius, *op. cit.*, p.46.
113. The recollections are from an untraced lecture Wood gave in Birmingham in 1900.
114. J.L.J. Masse, *The Art-Workers' Guild 1884–1934* (Oxford, Shakespeare Head Press, 1935) p.29.
115. Muthesius, *op. cit.*, p.55.
116. Drury, *op. cit.*, p.199.
117. *The British Architect, op. cit.*
118. Jewson, *op. cit.*, p.42.
119. Peter Davey, *Architecture of the Arts and Crafts Movement* (London, Architectural Press, 1980).
120. Drury, *op. cit.*, p.87.
121. Weaver, *op. cit.*, p.18.
122. A. Carruthers, M. Greensted, and B. Roscoe, *Ernest Gimson; Arts and Crafts Designer and Architect* (London, Yale University Press, 2019) p.149.
123. Weaver, *op. cit.*, p.20.
124. May Morris (ed.), *The Collected Works of William Morris* (London, 1914) vol. 20, p.20.
125. William Hesketh Lever, *The Buildings Erected at Port Sunlight and Thornton Hough* (Port Sunlight, 1902).
126. *The Studio*, vol. xxiv, 1902, p.168.
127. Raymond Unwin, *Cottage Plans and Common Sense* (London, 1902) p.9.
128. Jewson, *op. cit.*, p.33.
129. W.R. Lethaby, 'Town Tidying', in *Form in Civilization* (London, 1922) p.21.
130. Christopher Hussey, *The Life of Sir Edwin Lutyens* (London, 1950) p.187.
131. Quoted on http://www.ideal-homes.org.uk/case-studies/progress-estate (accessed 22 May 2018).
132. Susan Beattie, *A Revolution in London Housing; L.C.C. Housing Architects and Their Work, 1893–1914* (London, 1980) p.106.

This is not meant to be a comprehensive list but covers many of the architects and associated topics covered in this book.

Jill Allibone, *George Devey: Architect 1820–1886* (Cambridge, Lutterworth Press, 1991).

Clive Aslet, *The Edwardian Country House: A Social and Architectural History* (London, 2012).

Susan Beattie, *Revolution in London Housing* (London, The Architectural Press, 1980).

Phillada Ballard (ed.), *Birmingham's Victorian and Edwardian Architects* (Wetherby, Oblong Creative, 2009).

Geoff Brandwood and Rebecca Daniels (eds.), *Ruskin and Architecture* (Reading, Spire Books, 2003).

John Burnett, *Housing: A Social History, 1815–1970* (London, Methuen, 1978).

Annette Carruthers et al., *Ernest Gimson: Arts & Crafts Designer and Architect* (London, Yale University Press, 2019).

David Cole, *Sir Edwin Lutyens: The Arts and Crafts House* (Victoria, Image Publishing, 2020).

Martin Cook, *Edward Prior: Arts and Crafts Architect* (Marlborough, The Crowood Press, 2015).

Peter Cormack, *Arts and Crafts Stained Glass* (London, Yale University Press, 2015).

John Cornforth, *In Search of a Style: Country Life and Architecture, 1897–1935* (London, Andre Deutsch, 1988).

Alan Crawford, *C.R. Ashbee: Architect, Designer and Romantic Socialist* (London, Yale University Press, 2005).

Peter Davey, *Arts and Crafts Architecture: The Search for Earthly Paradise* (London, The Architectural Press, 1982).

Roger Dixon and Stefan Muthesius, *Victorian Architecture* (London, Thames & Hudson, 1993).

Michael Drury, *Wandering Architects: In Pursuit of an Arts and Crafts Ideal* (Stamford, Shaun Tyas Press, 2000).

Mark Girouard, *The Victorian Country House* (London, Yale University Press, 1985).

Mark Girouard, *Sweetness and Light: The 'Queen Anne' Movement, 1860–1900* (Oxford, The Clarendon Press, 1977).

Roderick Gradidge, *Dream Houses: The Edwardian Ideal* (London, Constable, 1980).

A. Stuart Gray, *Edwardian Architecture: A Biographical Dictionary* (London, Duckworth, 1985).

Hilary J. Grainger, *The Architecture of Sir Ernest George* (Reading, Spire Books, 2011).

Diane Haigh, *Baillie Scott: The Artistic House* (Chichester, John Wiley and Sons, 2004).

Michael Hall, *George Frederick Bodley and the Later Gothic Revival in Britain and America* (London, Yale University Press, 2014).

Alec Hamilton, *Arts and Crafts Churches* (London, Lund Humphries, 2020).

Robert Hewison, *Ruskin and his Contemporaries* (London, 2018).

Rosemary Hill, *God's Architect: Pugin and the Building of Romantic Britain* (London, 2007).

Wendy Hitchmough, *C.F.A. Voysey* (London, Phaidon, 1995).

Julian Holder and Elizabeth McKellar (eds.), *Neo-Georgian Architecture, 1880–1970: A Reappraisal* (Swindon, Historic England, 2016).

Sheila Kirk, *Philip Webb: Pioneer of Arts and Crafts Architecture* (Chichester, John Wiley and Sons, 2005).

James D. Kornwolf, *M.H. Baillie Scott and the Arts and Crafts Movement* (Baltimore, John Hopkins University Press, 1972).

Fiona MacCarthy, *William Morris: A Life for Our Time* (London, Faber & Faber, 1994).

Cyndy Manton, *Henry Wilson* (Cambridge, Lutterworth Press, 2009).

C. Miele (ed.), *From William Morris: Building Conservation and the Arts and Crafts Cult of Authenticity, 1877–1939* (London, Yale University Press, 2005).

Mervyn Miller, *Raymond Unwin: Garden Cities and Town Planning* (Leicester, Leicester University Press, 1992).

Gillian Naylor, *The Arts and Crafts Movement* (London, Trefoil, 1990).

Frederick O'Dwyer, *The Architecture of Deane & Woodward* (Cork, Cork University Press, 1997).

Bernard Porter, *The Battle of the Styles: Society, Culture and the Design of a New Foreign Office, 1855–61* (London, Continuum, 2011).

Godfrey Rubens, *William Richard Lethaby* (London, The Architectural Press, 1986).

Andrew Saint, *Richard Norman Shaw* (London, Yale University Press, 2010).

Alastair Service, *Edwardian Architecture: A Handbook to Building Design in Britain, 1890–1914* (London, Thames & Hudson, 1977).

Gavin Stamp, *Edwin Lutyens: Country Houses* (London, Country Life, 2001).

Peter Stansky, *Re-designing the World: William Morris, the 1880s and the Arts and Crafts* (Princeton, Princeton University Press, 1985).

Anthony Sutcliffe, *Towards the Planned City: Germany, Britain, the United States and France, 1780–1914* (Oxford, Blackwells, 1981).

Mark Swenarton, *Homes Fit for Heroes: The Politics and Architecture of Early State Housing* (London, Heineman, 1981).

Paul Thompson, *William Butterfield* (London, Routledge & Kegan Paul, 1971).

David Valinsky, *An Architect Speaks: The Writings and Buildings of Edward Schröder Prior* (Stamford, Shaun Tyas Press, 2015).

Adam Voelcker, *Herbert Luck North: Arts and Crafts Architecture for Wales* (Cardiff, Royal Commission on the Ancient and Historical Monuments of Wales, 2011).

The following is a list of places to stay, and places to visit, for those who want to take the subject further. Many of the buildings mentioned in the book are private houses; no right of access should be assumed and the owners' right to privacy respected. The list here is of places that are open to the public. However do check before visiting. The Garden Cities, estates and model villages such as Bedford Park, Port Sunlight, Bourneville, New Earswick, Brentham, Letchworth and Hampstead Garden Suburb remain as much a pleasure to walk around today; most will have places to stay if searched for.
All information was correct at the time of publication.

## PLACES TO STAY
### Cornwall
Porth-en-Alls, Prussia Cove. Available for self-catering.
https://prussiacove.co.uk

### Cumbria
The Abbey House Hotel, Barrow-in-Furness.
www.abbeyhousehotel.com
Broadleys, Lake Windermere. Now owned by the Windermere Motor Boat Racing Club – six bedrooms available.
www.wmbrc.co.uk
Cragwood Country House Hotel, Windermere. www.lakedistrict-countryhotels.co.uk/cragwood-hotel
The Eyrie, Brantwood. Self-catering apartment overlooking Coniston Water. www.brantwood.org.uk

### Devon
The Beach House, Exmouth.
www.thebeachhouseexmouth.co.uk
Winsford Cottage Hospital, Beaworthy. A unique holiday home for up to six people.
www.landmarktrust.org.uk

### Gloucestershire
The Bear of Rodborough, Stroud.
www.cotswold-inns-hotels.co.uk
Drakestone House, Stinchcombe.
https://drakestonehouse.co.uk
Forthampton Court, Forthampton. Self-catering accommodation.
https://big-cottages.com
Owlpen Manor, Uley.
www.owlpen.com
The Stonehouse Court Hotel, Stonehouse.
www.stonehousecourt.co.uk

### Hampshire
Avon Tyrrell, Bransgore.
www.avontyrrell.org.uk

### Herefordshire
Perrycroft, Upper Colwall. Three holiday cottages.
www.perrycroft.co.uk

### Kent
The Grange, Ramsgate. Self-catering holidays.
www.landmarktrust.org.uk

### Norfolk
The Pleasaunce, Overstrand. A Christian Endeavour Holiday Centre.
www.cehc.org.uk
Voewood, High Kelling.
www.voewood.com

### Northamptonshire
Groom Cottage, Ashby St Ledgers.
www.airbnb.co.uk/rooms/29664708

### North Yorkshire
The Prior's Lodge, Mount Grace Priory, Northallerton.
www.english-heritage.org.uk

### Northumberland
Whalton Manor, Whalton.
https://big-cottages.com

### South Yorkshire
The Parsonage House, Thurlstone.
www.airbnb.co.uk

### Surrey
Goddards, Abinger Common.
www.landmarktrust.org.uk/

## PLACES TO VISIT
### Cheshire
Lady Lever Art Gallery, Port Sunlight, Lower Road, Port Sunlight, Bebington, Wirral CH62 5EQ.
www.liverpoolmuseums.org.uk/lady-lever-art-gallery
Philharmonic Dining Rooms, 36 Hope Street, Liverpool L1 9BX.
www.nicholsonspubs.co.uk

### Cumbria
Blackwell, Bowness-on-Windermere LA23 3JT.
www.blackwell.org.uk
Brantwood, Coniston LA21 8AD.
www.brantwood.org.uk
Naworth Castle, Naworth, Brampton CA8 2HF. Usually only open by special arrangement.
www.naworth.co.uk
St Martin's Church, Front Street, Brampton CA8 1SH.
www.stmartinsbrampton.org.uk

Tullie House Museum and Art Gallery, Castle St, Carlisle CA3 8TP. www.tulliehouse.co.uk

**Dorset**
Holy Trinity Church, 101 Crock Lane, Bothenhampton, Bridport DT6 4BH.

**County Durham**
St Andrew's church, Talbot Rd, Roker, Sunderland SR6 9PT. https://monkwearmouthcofe.com

**East Sussex**
Standen, West Hoathly Road, East Grinstead RH19 4NE. www.nationaltrust.org.uk

**Gloucestershire**
All Saints' Church, Selsley, Stroud GL5 5LE.
http://allsaintsselsley.org.uk
Court Barn Museum, North Gate Lodge, Church Street, Chipping Campden GL55 6JE.
https://www.courtbarn.org.uk
Snowshill Manor, Snowshill, Broadway WR12 7JU.
www.nationaltrust.org.uk
The Church of St Edward the Confessor, Kempley, Dymock GL18 2BU.
The Wilson, Clarence Street, Cheltenham, GL50 3JT.
www.cheltenhammuseum.org.uk

**Herefordshire**
All Saints' Church, 3 The Parks, Brockhampton, Hereford HR1 4SD.
www.allsaintsbrockhampton.org

**Kent**
Red House, Red House Lane, London, Bexleyheath DA6 8JF.
www.nationaltrust.org.uk
Lancashire
Long Street Methodist Church, 93 Long Street, Middleton, M24 6UN.
https://artsandcraftschurch.org
The Ruskin, Lancaster University, Bailrigg, Lancaster LA1 4YH.
www.lancaster.ac.uk/the-ruskin

**Leicestershire**
New Walk Museum and Art Gallery, 53 New Walk, Leicester LE1 7EA.

www.leicester.gov.uk/leisure-and-culture/museums-and-galleries
Stoneywell, Whitcroft's Lane, Markfield LE67 9QE.
www.nationaltrust.org.uk
London
The Blackfriar, 174 Queen Victoria St, London EC4V 4EG.
www.nicholsonspubs.co.uk
Emery Walker's house, 7 Hammersmith Terrace, Hammersmith, London W6 9TS.
www.emerywalker.org.uk
The Tabard, 2 Bath Road, Turnham Green, London W4 1LW.
www.greeneking-pubs.co.uk
The Victoria and Albert Museum, Cromwell Road, Knightsbridge, London SW7 2RL. https://www.vam.ac.uk/
The William Morris Gallery, Lloyd Park, Forest Road, Walthamstow, London E17 4PP.
www.wmgallery.org.uk
North Yorkshire
Goddards, 27 Tadcaster Road, Dringhouses, York YO24 1GG.
www.nationaltrust.org.uk
St Martin-on-the-Hill, Albion Road, Scarborough YO11 2BT.
www.friendsofstmartins.co.uk

**Oxfordshire**
Ashmolean Museum, Beaumont Street, Oxford OX1 2PH.
www.ashmolean.org
Great Coxwell Barn, The Hollow Rd, Great Coxwell, Faringdon, SN7 7LZ.
www.nationaltrust.org.uk
Kelmscott Manor, Lechlade GL7 3HJ.
www.sal.org.uk/kelmscott-manor
Oxford University Museum of Natural History, Parks Road, Oxford OX1 3PW.
www.oumnh.ox.ac.uk

**South Yorkshire**
Millennium Gallery, Arundel Gate, Sheffield, S1 2PP.
www.museums-sheffield.org.uk/museums/millennium-gallery
Staffordshire
Wightwick Manor, Wightwick Bank, Wolverhampton WV6 8EE.
www.nationaltrust.org.uk